graphics

RotoVision

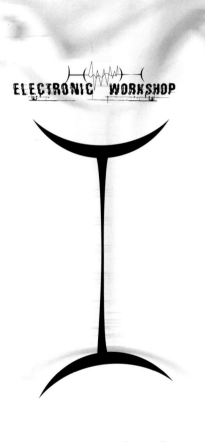

ELECTRONIC WORKSHOP

graphics

Real-world graphic design projects – from brief to finished solution

paul murphy

A ROTOVISION BOOK, PUBLISHED AND DISTRIBUTED BY ROTOVISION SA, RUE DU BUGNON 7, CH-1299 CRANS-PRÈS-CÉLIGNY, SWITZERLAND. ROTOVISION SA, SALES & PRODUCTION OFFICE, SHERIDAN HOUSE, 112/116A WESTERN ROAD, HOVE, EAST SUSSEX BN3 1DD, UK. TEL: +44 (0) 1273 72 72 68, FAX: +44 (0) 1273 72 72 69. DISTRIBUTED TO THE TRADE IN THE UNITED STATES BY: WATSON-GUPTILL PUBLICATIONS, 1515 BROADWAY, NEW YORK, NY 10036.

CONTENTS

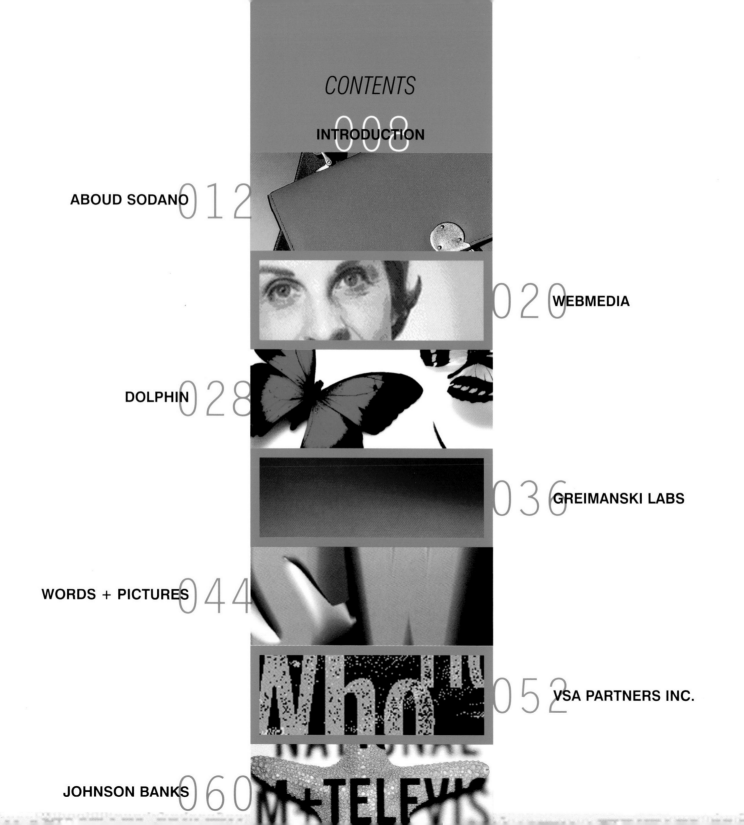

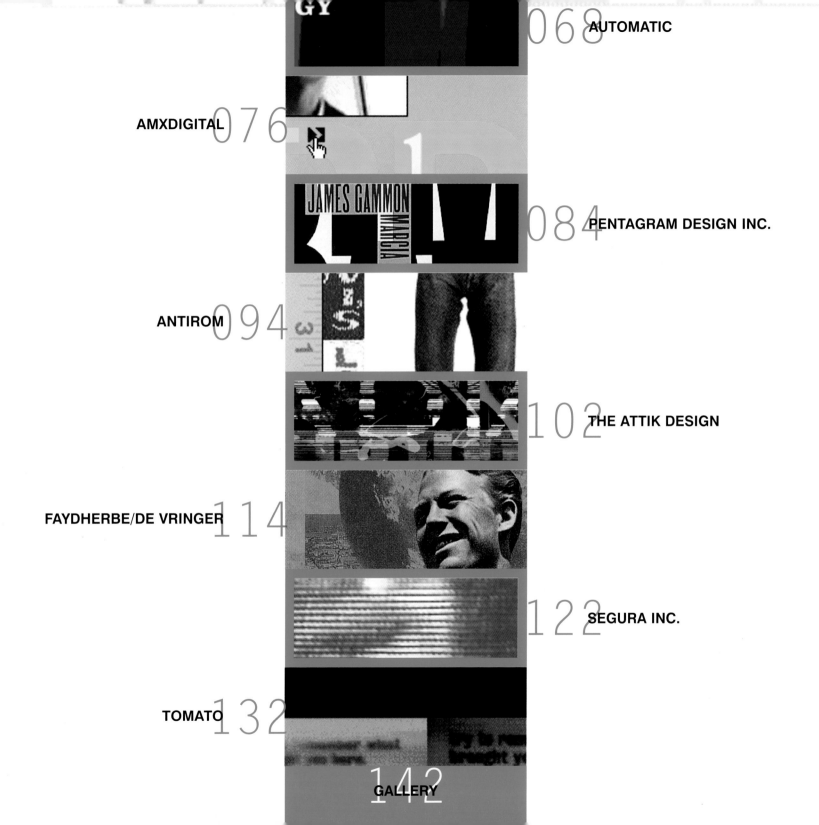

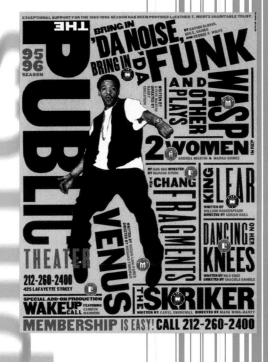

GRAPHICS, THE FIRST TITLE IN THE
ELECTRONIC WORKSHOP SERIES,
FEATURES THE WORK OF 15 DESIGN
COMPANIES WORKING ACROSS THE
SPECTRUM FROM WEB SITE DESIGN TO
PRINT-BASED DESIGN. THE PREMISE OF
THE BOOK IS THAT THE PROCESS
INVOLVED IN THE EVOLUTION OF A
PROJECT IS THE PART THAT REMAINS
UNSEEN, BUT THAT THIS IS WHERE THE
WORKINGS OF THE DESIGNER ARE MOST
REVEALING.

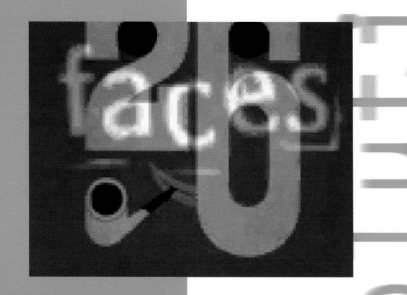

THE 15 SECTIONS THAT MAKE UP THE BODY OF THIS BOOK EACH FOCUS ON THE PROCESS OF A SINGLE PROJECT. IF THERE'S ANYTHING TO BE DRAWN BY COMPARING THE METHODS, THEN IT'S SIMPLY THAT THERE IS NO SIMPLE OR SINGLE FORMULA FOR SUCCESS.

WHY THE ELECTRONIC WORKSHOP? THE RISE OF THE DESKTOP COMPUTER IN THE MIDDLE OF THE 1980s HAS CHANGED THE WORKINGS OF GRAPHIC DESIGN. WHILE IT'S RARE TO FIND A STUDIO THAT DOESN'T INVOLVE A COMPUTER SOMEWHERE IN THE PROCESS, THE MESSAGE OF THIS BOOK IS THAT TECHNOLOGY WILL NEVER BE A SUBSTITUTE FOR CREATIVITY OR IDEAS. THE TRUISM THAT THE 'COMPUTER IS SIMPLY A TOOL' IS TRUER HERE THAN ANYWHERE ELSE. WHAT IT HAS BROUGHT IS A FLEXIBILITY AND AN ABILITY TO REALIZE THE VISION OF THE DESIGNER. IF DESIGN WERE SIMPLY ABOUT A MASTERY OF THE APPROPRIATE SOFTWARE, THEN WE COULD ALL BE DESIGNERS. WE ARE NOT, AND THE PROCESS IS NEVER THAT SIMPLE. WHAT IS REFLECTED IN *GRAPHICS* IS THE DIVERSITY OF MEANINGS, MESSAGES AND METHODS. AS MUCH AS THIS BOOK TRIES TO UNRAVEL THE ELEMENTS OF A SUCCESSFUL DESIGN AND DESIGN PRACTICE, IT ALSO ALLOWS US A PARTIAL SNAPSHOT OF THE CURRENT STATE OF GRAPHIC DESIGN.

THE SELECTION CRITERIA FOR THE DESIGNERS
INCLUDED IN THE BOOK WAS ONE OF DIVERSITY ALLIED
TO OUTSTANDING WORK. A BRIEF WAS SENT TO
DESIGNERS WITH QUESTIONS ABOUT THE DESIGN
PROCESS AND A REQUEST FOR VISUALS TO REPRESENT
THAT. THE INFORMATION WAS COLLECTED THROUGH
INTERVIEWS, FROM DESIGNERS' STATEMENTS, FROM
LETTERS, FAXES AND E-MAIL BOUNCING BACKWARDS
AND FORWARDS. DESIGNERS TALKED AND WROTE
ABOUT WHAT WAS IMPORTANT TO THEM IN THE
PROCESS, ABOUT DESIGN AND ITS RELATIONSHIP TO
TECHNOLOGY AND MUCH MORE. THE BOOK REFLECTS
THE RANGE OF THAT WORK, AS WELL AS THE METHODS
AND RESPONSES.

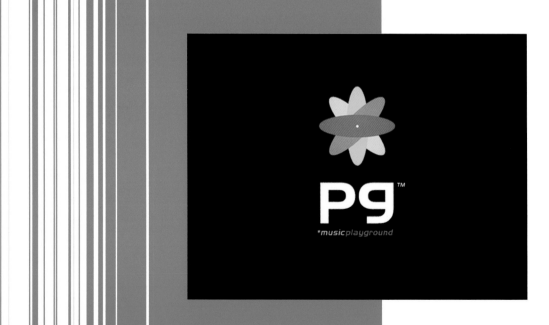

CD-ROM
D&AD
Awards
Search
Sponsors

Exit

1. ABOUD SODANO
ADVERTS FOR PAUL SMITH BAGS

THE APPROACH:
MANY DESIGNERS LOOKING AT THESE ADVERTS FOR PAUL SMITH BAGS WOULD ASSUME THAT THEY WERE THE RESULT OF BRINGING TOGETHER THE VARIOUS ELEMENTS IN PHOTOSHOP. IN REALITY THE COMPLEXITY HAS BEEN ACHIEVED ON A SINGLE TRANSPARENCY IN THE CAMERA WITH THE COMPUTER BEING USED ONLY AT THE END FOR RETOUCHING AND TO ADD THE FINAL TEXT.

Paul Smith
BAG

MANUFACTURED AND DISTRIBUTED BY YOSHINAGA CORPORATION
INFORMATION: PAUL SMITH JAPAN 03-3486 1500

AD:ABOUD PHOTOGRAPHY:SODANO

BACKGROUND TO THE COMPANY:

Alan Aboud and Sandro Sodano are graduates in graphics from St Martin's in London and have a client list that includes Calvin Klein, Issey Miyake and the Terence Higgins Trust. 'In 1990 there was such a proliferation of work heading down the computer route that when we started up we decided that we would focus on having very, very strong ideas and that would be our driving force. The thing about computers is that technically the possibilities really are limitless, whereas photography does have limits and for us it's about exploiting the strengths and weaknesses of photography as a medium,' says Sandro Sodano. Alan Aboud has been art director for Paul Smith Limited, responsible for the presentation of all Paul Smith lines, since 1990.

PROJECT CREDITS

ART DIRECTOR: ALAN ABOUD
PHOTOGRAPHY: SANDRO SODANO

THE PROJECT:

The ideas for all the Paul Smith accessory pictures tend to come from the product itself, they're never 'lifestyle' types of pictures but draw more on the visual wit and humour that makes up Paul Smith's appeal.

'The main directive, if there is one, from Paul Smith is that one must try and get humour into everything. Not slapstick, but it's not a po-faced brand and that's its inner strength,' says Alan Aboud. 'There's never a brief as such. We usually don't know what we're going to do until the products arrive. If you like, the brief is what's inside the cardboard box and what's the best thing to do with it.'

The brief is what's inside the cardboard box. The bags themselves determine the approach.

INITIAL IDEAS:

The Spring/Summer '97 collection marked the advent of the first line of women's bags. The difficulty was that there wasn't a single unifying theme to the bags' design that could be carried across a series of adverts. Each was quite different to the others so any advertising had to stand on its own, but also be understood as part of a range.

One initial idea focused on the brightly-coloured linings and, according to Sandro Sodano, various test shots were made 'simply to see what we could do with lighting and colour. That was the first stage and it showed us that an idea that would work on one bag wouldn't necessarily work with the others. We also tried out the idea of showing the bags open and closed in a single shot, but weren't keen on them. We were a bit stuck then.'

1 Previous adverts have taken the idea of bags as being something to carry objects from place to place (Autumn/Winter '94);

2 from the contents of bags (Spring/Summer '96);

3 and bags as soft, squashy things (Autumn/Winter '96).

An earlier project, the invites for the Tenjikai wholesale show in Japan where buyers would see the bags for the first time, finally provided the idea from which the project evolved.

'In the case of the Tenjikai invite, we wanted to do something very simple with the bags. And at that stage we were working from the designer's sketches so it wouldn't have been possible to photograph them anyway. One of the important things about this line is that it marked the launch of the women's line of bags. We just hit upon the idea of "men's" and "women's" at its most basic level – '70s toilet signs. Images were first scanned from a book of clip art. The bags were then drawn in and the graduated fills added to create the image for the invite.'

'We'd toyed with the idea of not using photography, however, time was running out so we decided to give it one last shot, having talked ideas for ages,' says Alan Aboud. 'In the end, the final project – from realization to delivery – took less than a week and we're still very happy with it, which isn't always the case. It might not sound a very professional way of working but we're honest about it. We're very lucky about working so closely together because the ideas feed off each other – it's not like an art director giving a photographer a sketch, but more a mutually creative process.'

Paul Smith
BAG

MANUFACTURED AND DISTRIBUTED BY YOSHINAGA CORPORATION
INFORMATION: PAUL SMITH JAPAN 03-3486 1500

AD:ABOUD PHOTOGRAPHY:SODANO

'THE KEY TO A LOT OF WHAT WE DO IS TO LEAVE WELL ALONE AND NOT TO USE THE TECHNOLOGY FOR THE SAKE OF IT. LESS IS MORE.'

Alan Aboud.

SOFTWARE/HARDWARE

QUARKXPRESS
PAINTBOX
POWERMACS

WORKING PROCESS

THE MAJORITY OF TIME INVOLVED IN THE PROJECT WAS SPENT DEVELOPING THE IDEA THAT WOULD ULTIMATELY FORM THE SERIES OF ADVERTS. WHILE IT LEFT LITTLE TIME BEFORE THE DEADLINE FOR COMPLETION, IT MEANT THAT THE ACTUAL PRACTICAL PROCESS OF MAKING THE WORK WAS RELATIVELY STRAIGHTFORWARD AS THE KEY CONCEPTS HAD ALREADY BEEN ARRIVED AT IN THEIR FINAL FORM.

ABOUD SODANO
STUDIO 7 • 10/11 ARCHER STREET • SOHO
LONDON W1V 7HG • UK

CLIENTS INCLUDE: *Art direction/design*: Terrence
Higgins Trust; Design Museum, London; Issey Miyake,
Japan; Sony Music. *Photography*: British Telecom; Conde
Nast; Macys, New York; Calvin Klein. **[SEE PAGE 143]**

2. WEBMEDIA
THE YOUTHNET SITE

Netscape: The Site

Back | Forward | Home | Reload | Images | Open | Print | Find | Stop | AltaVista

tsite: http://www.thesite.org.uk/

[SEARCH]

S

in

out of

SITE

[MAGAZINE]

?

[MAP]

about us . . .
with thanks to . . .
legal disclaimer . . .

Document : Done.

WEBMEDIA was set up in late 1994 by Ivan Pope and Steve Bowbrick in London. The founding of Webmedia was based on the belief that while many people were offering Web design services, few understood the full strategic implications of designing and maintaining a site for a client. The company now numbers 35 staff members and their clients range from the BBC and Sony, to Lufthansa and Reader's Digest.

COMPANY BACKGROUND:

WEBDEVELOPMENT was founded by Ben Hayman and Stephen Hebditch in March of 1996. In partnership with Webmedia, Webdevelopment was able to offer a combined technical and design approach to YouthNet. Webdevelopment produces software products to allow a site's administrators to handle large amounts of information which requires continuous updating and republishing.

PROJECT CREDITS:

DESIGN: NEIL CLAVIN
WEB SITE PRODUCER: DAMIAN RAFFERTY

WEBDEVELOPMENT: BEN MIDDLETON
                                 BEN HAYMAN
                                 STEPHEN HEBDITCH

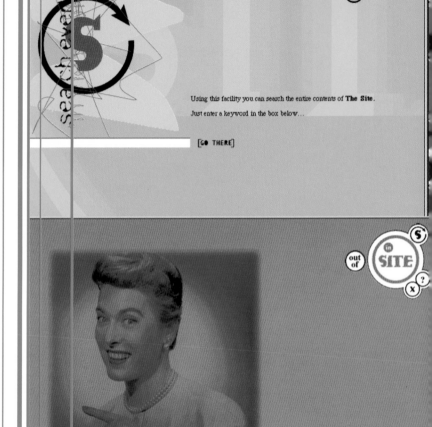

Using this facility you can search the entire contents of **The Site**.

Just enter a keyword in the box below...

[GO THERE]

THE BRIEF:

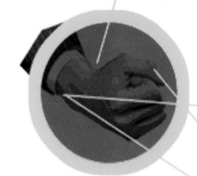

YouthNet is a registered UK charity which is involved in providing information and advice for young people 'before taking decisions that will affect the rest of their lives'.

The emphasis is on providing information on a practical basis. Hence there is an emphasis on enabling the site's users to contact organizations that are local to their area. This is accessible through a database searchable by criteria, from subject through to postcode.

FROM THE YOUTHNET SITE:

'THE SITE IS A WHOLE NEW KIND OF SIGNPOST. IT WILL BECOME THE FIRST STEP FOR ANYBODY LOOKING FOR AN OPPORTUNITY, HELP OR ADVICE ON A WIDE RANGE OF TOPICS ANYWHERE IN THE UK. OUR AIM IS TO HELP YOU QUICKLY FIND THE RIGHT ORGANIZATION IN THE RIGHT PLACE, WHATEVER YOU ARE LOOKING FOR.'

'MY FEELING IS THAT YOU MIGHT NEVER ARRIVE AT THIS IF YOU WERE DOING IT ALL ON THE COMPUTER.' Sandro Sodano.

THE PROCESS:

The first stage involved suspending the bags with fine wires in front of a white background with a model between the background and the bag. The models were chosen from Paul Smith's staff. The silhouette of the figure is shot first which gives the clean white background. Then, with the model out of the way, graduated colour is shot on to the backdrop. Where the figure had been blocking the light out, the transparency picks up the second colour while the area around it, having already been exposed to the bright white background, remains white. At this stage the bag still had not been exposed, itself appearing as a silhouette. Lastly the bag is lit, completing the image.

'It became a selection process of who we used and how they posed to give the bags a personality without changing them a great deal. If you look at the Polaroids you can see all the different things we tried out. It's a lengthy process because you have to do all three stages before you can see what it looks like. In some, we hinted at the idea that the model might be holding the bag but ultimately we weren't too precious about that,' says Sandro Sodano.

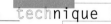
technique

This project demonstrates the significance of a strong idea over any kind of computer gimmickry. While it might seem that a similar result could have been obtained more easily on an all-digital path, the final result fully justifies the decision to work in camera. Here, the computer is no more than one tool used alongside many to complete the work.

AD:ABOUD PHOTOGRAPHY:SODANO

Final retouching was done on a Quantel Paintbox and the original 5 x 4 inch transparencies were output as 10 x 8 inch transparencies. The strings were taken out and any imperfections removed from the bags. The final text was added using a Macintosh and QuarkXPress. In keeping with the overall style of Paul Smith's advertising, the typography is very minimal with the image carrying the weight of the message.

'My feeling is that you might never arrive at this if you were doing it all on the computer. If I knew that the only way of doing this was by creating it on the computer, I probably wouldn't have bothered to go as far as we did. It might work for other people but this way of allowing it to evolve works for us,' says

Sandro Sodano. 'It's not about saying "because we can do it on a camera we're so clever" – the end result is what matters. For us, this kind of picture-taking is part of the design process.'

'The result is achieved in the photographic studio and that's what you get in the end. I find it much more gratifying to realize an image from one transparency than to go into a paintbox suite and scan in 20 images to make one. Some designers can do that to great effect but I can't.

I wish I could because it'd be faster for me. The one time me and Sandro tried that it was an unmitigated disaster, it looked really boring. The spontaneity and uncertainty you get with the way we work is the joy of it,' says Alan Aboud.

out of | in SITE | S | x | ?

Woodcraft Folk

0171 672 6031

Woodcraft Folk activities are based around weekly group meetings for both boys and girls. Groups are divided into four age ranges: Elfins 6-9 year olds, Pioneers - 10-12 year olds, Venturers - 13-25 year olds and District Fellowship - 16-20 year olds. Programmes may include games, drama, singing, dancing, craftwork, discussion and projects. Groups regularly hike, amp an denjoy other residential experiences. International understanding is an importnat part of the curriculum, which is supported by a large exchange programme.

Costs/waiting lists   Weekly subscription up to 16 is 40-50p. 16-17 annual subscription is £5 unwaged. 16+ unwaged is £8, waged £15

Address   13 Ritherdon Road
London
SW17 8QE

Telephone   0181 767 9799

Fax   0181 767 2457

E-mail   folk_hou@woodcrft.demon.co.uk

Web site   http://www.poptel.org.uk/woodcraft

Region served   UK

Special needs   All groups encourage full participation by all members of the community

Neil Clavin, graphic designer, Webmedia:
'The brief was to create a template-driven environment for an information database targeted at 12–35 year olds dealing with matters that affect them. The client's previous site had been deemed too worthy and as a consequence likely to be off-putting to the people they were trying to reach. Key questions that needed to be tackled were the structuring and promotion of the site.'

While within the site its significance is the information it contains, it needs to be housed within an engaging and easily understood interface. The material is broadly split into categories such as drugs, housing and homelessness, sex, health, money, free time, education and training. Alongside the information database the site would comprise an online magazine which could be easily updated by staff at YouthNet, a section about YouthNet, its sponsors and partners, and a search facility and help area.

There are also plans in the future to have the site installed at an outdoor interactive kiosk in central London so that people who do not have Internet access (the homeless) will not be excluded from the site.

THE INITIAL APPROACH:

'We used the sort of corporate branding that permeates fashion and the idea of creating a "channel" called the "SITE". This logo also became a global navigation device to move between the sections such as database (InSite) and magazine (OutofSite). In this way, the logo became both branding and navigation device – sitting like an MTV logo in the top right-hand corner.'

'The navigation bar for InSite (the main database) was made to look throw-away, as if it was a photocopy ripped out, with a hard and nasty red biro/spray-can highlighting which section had been selected.' Neil Clavin.

ADVICE   DRUGS   EDUCATION   FREETIME   HEALTH   HOUSING   MONEY   SEX   SPORT   WORK

Drugs search results

E9

ORGANISATIONS
Brixton Drug Project (9.8 km)

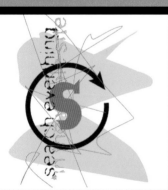

'THE IDEAS WERE BASED ON THE FEELING OF BEING YOUNG, QUITE PROBABLY WITH VERY LITTLE MONEY IN THE OFTEN HOSTILE URBAN ENVIRONMENTS OF THE 90s AND HOW THAT COULD BE COMMUNICATED, WHILE STILL BEING EMPATHIC – IDEAS OF WASTED LOW-TECH SECOND-HAND AND DIY GLAMOUR, CONCRETE, FOUND OBJECTS AND GRAFFITI, ANGULARITY AND DISINTEGRATION.' NEIL CLAVIN.

The information on the site is managed using Mediasurface, proprietary software developed by Webdevelopment. As a result, a small staff at YouthNet can maintain the content, allowing immediate and ongoing site updates. The site's content can be searched by various criteria, including subject and postcode, and thus can identify organizations local to individual users.

Netscape: The Site: About us

| Back | Forward | Home | | Reload | Images | Open | Print | Find | | Stop | AltaVista | | | N |

Netsite: `http://www.thesite.org.uk/aboutus.html`

out of SITE

ABOUT US

The Site is a whole new kind of signpost. It will become the first step for anybody looking for an opportunity, help or advice on a wide range of topics anywhere in the UK. Our aim is to help you quickly find the right organisation in the right place, whatever you are looking for.

We've had a test site up since November 1995. What we've learned is that you want to know not only the most relevant people who can help you, but the closest too - hence the emphasis on being able to find things locally.

The Site is produced and managed by YouthNet, a registered charity which thinks it's important that people have the best information and advice available before taking decisions that will affect the rest of their lives.

We are constantly adding new organisations and services to our system, with details of how to get in touch. But if there's a local group working with young people that you think we've missed out, then tell us and we'll get it online. Here's where you can do this. Or they can fill in an online form and send it to us. Here's where they can do that.

WHAT WE BELIEVE IN.. ▶

| About us | | [GO THERE] |

DEVELOPING THE IDEA:

'In the first designs there was some concern from the client that the imagery in the background would be thought of as being "clickable" and could create confusion. There was a definite wish on my part to include some sort of imagery in the background to lift the visual appearance of a project which would rely heavily on text-based information.'

'The client had suggested a pop art feel, possibly using some "Warhol-type imagery". To try to fit in with this, a range of pretty kitsch 1950s photographs were used, saturated in acidic colours and reduced as much as possible to keep file size and download times reasonable.' Neil Clavin.

technique

A GUIDE TO GOOD WEB DESIGN:
'Think carefully about the structuring of the site and how you would move through it in an intuitive way. Don't leave the structure up to someone else and slavishly provide graphics for something which may be fundamentally flawed from the beginning.'

'Think about feelings and atmosphere – how you want to feel as you progress through it. Don't think of it as a Web site or a page, think of it as: if at this point, before I have tried to design anything, what do I picture in my head that would be my idea of a brilliant piece of electronic information?'

'Don't think about the design as a collection of pages, it is what is between these "pages" which contributes to the whole.'

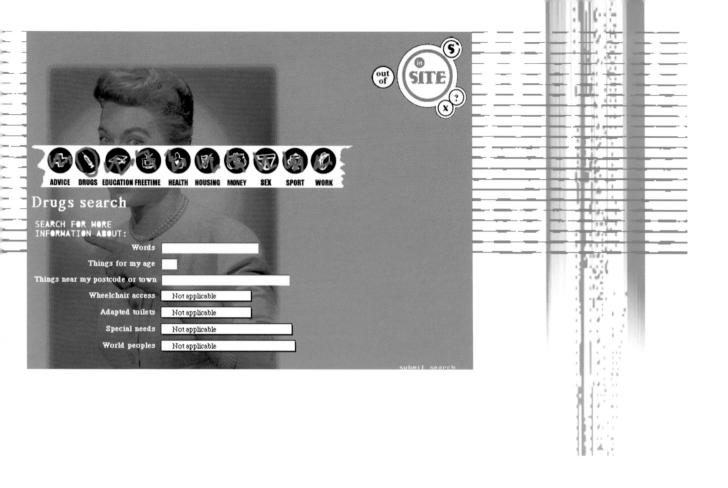

Drugs search

SEARCH FOR MORE
INFORMATION ABOUT:

Words	
Things for my age	
Things near my postcode or town	
Wheelchair access	Not applicable
Adapted toilets	Not applicable
Special needs	Not applicable
World peoples	Not applicable

submit search

'Learn, or at least understand, HTML so you know what you can and cannot do with your design without backing yourself into a corner.'

'Try and have a fairly Zen attitude concerning the positioning and alignment of elements and try to design them so that perhaps it doesn't matter that much that they don't align, that it's slightly more organic.'

'Ideas that fit together into the whole, not "hey, this is new, it must be good" software gimmickry.'

'In general don't look to the Web for inspiration, look at new ideas in print which question the validity of the page as an information medium – think of film, television title sequences and the structuring of retail environments. I think designers on the Web have a responsibility to try and extend the thinking which has shaped art, graphic design, philosophy and architecture into the digital environment.'
Neil Clavin, Webmedia.

SOFTWARE/HARDWARE

PHOTOSHOP 3.0
ILLUSTRATOR 5.5
GIF BUILDER
DEBABELISER
PICTIFY

WORKING PROCESS

AS NEIL CLAVIN SAYS OF THE DESIGN PROCESS INVOLVED IN WEB SITE DESIGN:

'START OFF WRITING THINGS DOWN ABOUT WHAT THE PURPOSE AND MAIN FUNCTION OF THE SITE IS AND HOW THIS CAN BE EXPRESSED GRAPHICALLY. THEN START

WORKING OUT THE STRUCTURE. THEN START MESSING ABOUT WITH SOME GRAPHIC IDEAS ON PAPER. THEN TRY IT ON A COMPUTER. THEN GO BACK TO WORKING IT OUT ON PAPER. AND AGAIN, AND AGAIN...'

WEBMEDIA
2 KENDALL PLACE • LONDON W1H 3AH • UK

CLIENTS INCLUDE: Which?; Time Out; Reader's Digest; BBC; Sony Music Europe. **[SEE PAGE 156]**

3. DOLPHIN
IDENTITY FOR RENAISSANCE

'FOR THE RENAISSANCE IDENTITY WE WERE LOOKING TO GET AWAY FROM CLUB-TYPE GRAPHICS, AND DOING SOMETHING SIMPLE, VERY MINIMAL, MORE A CASE OF EVOKING A FEELING. IT'S A COMPLETE REACTION AGAINST THE OVERWORKED, OVER-COLOURED, CLUBBY, CLUTTERED, TECHNO GRAPHICS THAT WERE AROUND AT THE TIME.'
ROB PETRIE, DOLPHIN.

The Renaissance Four packaging takes the move towards simplicity even further. Surprisingly for a piece of packaging design, there is no indication on the front of what it is. Instead, it relies on a total brand recognition or the mystery of an unlabelled package to initially entice the buyer. Details appear on the side of the box and the Renaissance logo does appear on the back but even here it's simply embossed, white on white.

PROJECT CREDITS

DESIGNERS: PHIL SIMS
                    ROB PETRIE

PHOTOGRAPHERS: MERTON GAUSTER
                    TOBY MCFARLAN-POND

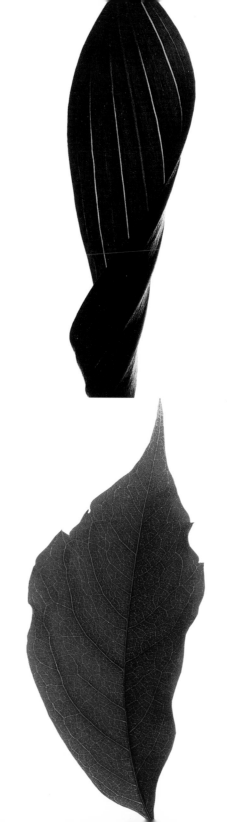

technique

Much interactive media, whether it's kiosk- or Web-based, ignores the fact that the average user only stays long enough to see a small fraction of the content. So it's crucial to a project's success that, however short a period a user stays, they retain a sense of satisfaction from the interaction.

THE BRIEF:

The client Renaissance was set up in early 1992 by club promoter Geoff Oakes who, as he himself says, 'had seen the best and the worst and was getting bored with the whole scene, and needed something new, something fresh.' The name Renaissance was chosen as it suggested the idea of rebirth for jaded clubbers. As such, early promotional work drew heavily on Renaissance imagery which quickly led to a host of imitators. At the time it approached Dolphin, Renaissance had worked with a range of designers and was looking for something new.

'The way we understand Renaissance is that it's a club for slightly older clubbers who might be a bit disillusioned with the dance scene. It's all about a quality package – from the CDs to the events,' says Dolphin's Phil Sims.

The brief involved producing material for all the Renaissance events: a monthly ad campaign in music and style magazines, a series of one-off dates around Britain, CD releases twice a year and events in Ibiza.

'IT WAS A CASE OF COMING UP WITH SOMETHING SUIT-ABLY CORPORATE FOR THE WHOLE THING BUT STILL ALLOWING INDIVIDUAL PARTS TO HAVE THEIR OWN IDENTITY. A LOT OF THE PREVIOUS WORK WAS QUITE LITERAL OF WHAT A CLUB IS OR WHAT THE NAME MEANS AND WE WANTED TO AVOID THAT.' Rob Petrie.

1

'We had to retain this very script-like font for the "R" which was the only stipulation from Renaissance. In the redesign, we made it very small and a bit more subtle and used it as a trademark type of logo. The font we used is Rotis, but we have tweaked the characters slightly. We've used Helvetica in six point for almost all the body copy, because it's simple yet informative.' Rob Petrie.

1

renaissance ®R

DEVELOPING THE IDEA:

Taking natural forms and objects as the theme, Dolphin worked on how it could be adapted into a highly recognizable visual style across the different areas of promotional material that Renaissance needed. In the ever-evolving world of club graphics it was important that it was distinctive from the competition. As Rob Petrie says: 'It was adaptable enough to fit the different areas of the campaign. Although ironically almost all the objects are dead, there's a warmer, more human, tactile feeling.' The first magazine advert came out at Easter and featured quail's eggs. The look is deliberately one that would more usually be associated with a perfume or high-fashion advert.

renaissance ®

The photography for the first campaign was carried out over a two-day period with photographer Merton Gauster. The objects were laid out on clean white backgrounds and the film was cross-processed – that is, shot on E6 slide film but processed as if it were a negative film using the C 41 process. The result is a shift in the colours and a slightly unreal feeling that works well on the printed page, keeping the texture in the shadows. The objects are photographed from the same angle with almost identical lighting so that although the pictures were used across a 12 month time-span, there is a sense of a single identity.

'We knew things were going well when the ad manager at the *Face* – which I suppose is still regarded as a bit of a style bible – would place the Renaissance ads at the front of the magazine alongside Comme de Garçon rather than the back with all the other club ads. I think it was when that happened that people really understood what we were after with the campaign,' says Rob Petrie.

The recent work, while still integrating in the overall campaign, marks a move towards an abstraction of forms. The photographs, taken this time by Toby McFarlan-Pond, are still taken on a white background but in the print they are reproduced on a warmer, off-white background. The packaging for Renaissance Four is a real opportunity for the designers to pursue the 'less-is-more' path.

'FOR US, IT'S GREAT HAVING A CLIENT LETTING US DO IT THE WAY WE THINK IT WORKS BEST. IT'S NOT THAT WE DON'T LIKE TYPOGRAPHY BUT OFTEN TEXT CAN SPOIL THE IMAGE.'

Despite having a very strong unified style, the identity allows enough flexibility to distinguish individual events within a season. For a series of clubs in Ibiza, this shot of a group of butterflies was used to promote the whole series and then individual shots were used to brand individual nights.

renaissance ®
ibiza 96

Renaissance at Pacha	DJ's	PA's	Wednesday 26th June	Tickets
Every Wednesday 26th June - 18th September 1996 Midnight - 7am	John Digweed Paul Oakenfold Fathers Of Sound Danny Rampling Jeremy Healy Dave Seaman Joe T Vannelli Little Louie Vega Ian Ossia Marc Auerbach Jon Pleased Wimmin TBC Alex Neri Nigel Dawson Chris & James Mark Tabberner	Bedrock Kym Mazelle Kamasutra Justine	Opening night in association with Mixmag John Digweed Fathers Of Sound Nigel Dawson	Advance tickets available from Renaissance 01782 717872/3 Kiwi Bar, San Antonio 1000 Pesatas discount and free drink with a Renaissance flyer Free coaches from San Antonio to Pacha 12.30am - 2.30am from Kiwi Bar and Café Del Mar Return coaches from Pacha to San Antonio 5am - 7am For further details of Renaissance at Pacha call 01782 717872/3
	Residents John Digweed Fathers Of Sound Ian Ossia None of the above DJ's are exclusive... But the club is!			

DESIGN AND TECHNOLOGY:

'When I'm knocking out ideas I need to work in a layout pad as working on the computer just isn't quick enough. Once I've got a page of sketches I take it to the Mac. Its strength is in the graphic solutions once you've got the big idea, but you can't come up with an identity solely on the Mac,' says Rob Petrie.

'You can spend more time on the details when you're working on the computer. Before the Mac, with pasting-up you could spend a few days just sticking down a record cover once you had actually finished the design itself,' agrees Phil Sims.

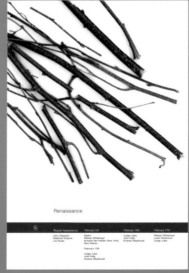
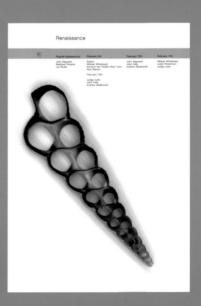
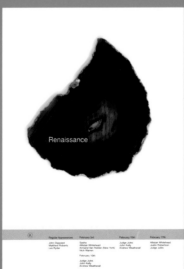

Early work produced for pitch ideas on the Renaissance identity.

'The main considerations with the CD packaging design was that as well as being visually attractive with real impact, it also had to be a lot more compact and user friendly. The new packaging had to compliment the new visual style and move away from the old fold-out format Renaissance had previously used. We sourced a variety of box samples from our suppliers and saw various elements on each box we liked. We'd adapt and specify certain things to the manufacturers and they'd make up samples for us, often overnight.'

'WE NEEDED TO COME UP WITH NEW IMAGERY FOR THE CD. IT'S MIXED BY THE FATHERS OF SOUND, AN ITALIAN DJ DUO, AND WE WERE BRIEFED THAT THERE WOULD BE THREE CDS IN THE PACK, BUT THAT WAS ABOUT IT. AS IT WAS TO BE RELEASED IN THE SUMMER WE USED THREE FLOWERS AND USED THE COLOURS OF THE ITALIAN FLAG.'

Again, the photography was by Merton Gauster and in the end the CD was produced in three different colours. 'The thing about using the three coloured designs was that they looked great in the record stores. It was another way of differentiating what we were trying to do from everything else.' Rob Petrie.

The CD packaging for Renaissance Three is constructed out of heavy-duty card. The clean elegant look is in stark contrast to the busy grunge look of much dance music packaging and promotion at the time.

SOFTWARE/HARDWARE

PHOTOSHOP
ILLUSTRATOR
FONTOGRAPHER
FREEHAND

DOLPHIN
32 NEAL STREET • COVENT GARDEN
LONDON • WC2H 9PS • UK

CLIENTS INCLUDE: Epic Records; Levi Strauss (UK) Ltd.; Harvey Nichols; Deconstruction Records.
[SEE PAGE 147]

4. GREIMANSKI LABS
LUX PICTURES IDENTITY

DESIGN DIRECTOR: APRIL GREIMAN
ASSISTANTS: NEAL IZUMI
                     LORNA TURNER

April Greiman has been highly influential in the area of digital design over the last 20 years. She was one of the first designers to recognize the potential of the early Macintoshes in creating a new language of imaging technology. 'Hybrid Imagery', a phrase coined by Greiman, best describes the unique synthesis of innovation, art and technology that her latest incarnation, the 'Greimanski Labs', produces.

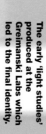

The early 'light studies' produced at the Greimanski Labs which led to the final identity.

BRIEF:

Founded in 1994 by producers James Magowan and Martin Kistler to develop and produce motion pictures, Lux Pictures currently has six projects in active development. April Greiman was hired to create an identity for the company based around the idea of the 'raw power of light'. The company will also collaborate with April Greiman on titles and graphics for a Web site, theatrical motion picture titles, and TV commercial graphics.

'We had done the start of a print campaign and even at that stage when I started working on the identity I knew that it would have applications to different media. In the logo the letters are different sizes and located in different planes to imply space and time. As soon as you have motion, which is what a movie company is about, you're implying both space and time.' April Greiman.

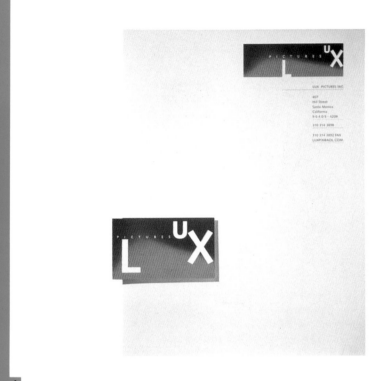

1

The first application for the Lux Pictures identity was in print. Here the themes of time, space and motion are implied in the design that is later carried through into the moving sequence and on to a Web site.

APPROACH:

'We studied and documented many different "light situations". Through the use of traditional photography and video we created "light phenomena" and then documented each using various media as appropriate. In this respect, and typically, we functioned as our own laboratory. This is the main approach of Greimanski Labs, both as a research lab and as an applied design lab.'

Netscape: LUX Pictures

Netsite: http://www.aprilgreiman.com/LUXPictures.html

PROJECTS

"LUX Pictures" 1995
Venice, CA
Identity + Motion graphics

home

2

The production of digital movies on the desktop can be easily managed by a small creative team. In this case, it's used as another expression of the client's identity, drawing on the original ideas that are developed in ways appropriate for each medium.

LuxCore

1318
Pacific Avenue
Venice
California
90291-3608
310 314 3898
FAX
310 314 3892

LUXCORE@AOL.COM

The Lux Pictures identity went on to be developed in a second variation for a new endeavour by the same client, Lux Core, a movie/media studio in Culver City.

'LIGHT IS PART OF A RANGE OF RADIATION KNOWN AS THE ELECTRO-MAGNETIC SPECTRUM. DIFFERENT PARTS OF THE SPECTRUM CONTAIN DIFFERENT AMOUNTS OF ENERGY: LOW ENERGY RADIO WAVES TO HIGHER GAMMA RAYS.'

LUX LOGO:

'The final image-symbols that I chose to present were three distinct light solutions that were in the primary colours (red, blue, yellow). These results/studies were presented as possible image-symbols for the client to choose from. These were then applied to various media, as deemed appropriate.'

'Each letter 'L', 'U', 'X' is seen as an individual 'light-object' in space. The image-symbol is a space in which a 'light-event' is occurring. Particular attention was paid to not using a typeface which was nostalgic/retro **in nature, as this is a traditional "Hollywood" movie company approach. We used the Syntax typeface for its contemporary, industrial, clean, yet quirky characteristics.' April Greiman.**

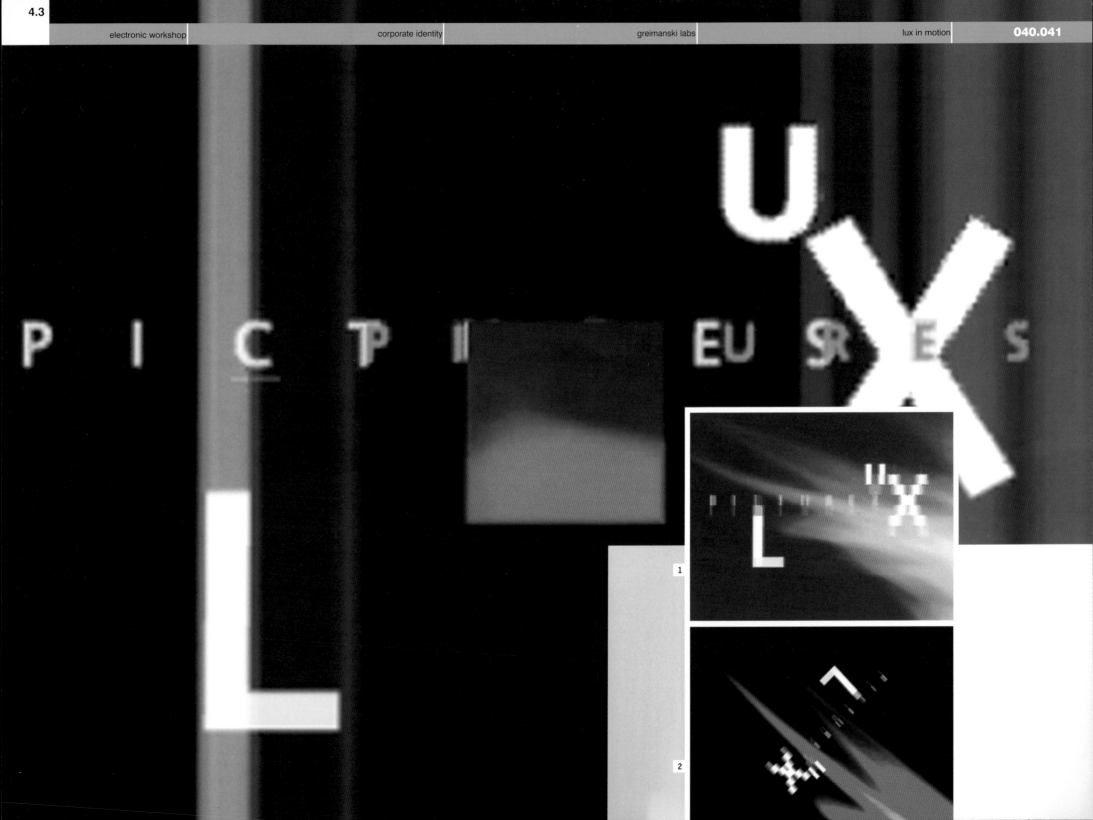

1 – 6

The individual frames from the Lux Pictures QuickTime movie produced by April Greiman in Adobe After Effects. The QuickTime movie is a study for the company's Web site. It's planned that the Web site will be a facility for direct public interaction with motion pictures, as well as keeping in touch with Lux Pictures distributors, writers, directors, and talent.

LUX IN MOTION:

'Movement of light through space is critical – it is fundamental in conveying that this is a space/ environment and not a two-dimensional page, particularly for the "Web version" of this movie.'

'The first image on the "movie loop" is the fire: the "original light", the flame. From space this primordial fire created the rest of the material world, including "Lux".'

'The element of time and creation is represented in the rotating letters of the name, or word, Lux. The graphic bar code/graphic/becomes spatial/space

over/in time. A goal here was to create a spatial image while using only two-dimensional elements. This is very important for "Web formats" for the Labs, as most clients and designers are referring to these spaces/ environments as "pages" and using very old nomenclature for the latest technological/electronic (r)evolution. We feel this is a mistake and that new terms need to be developed simultaneously with new tools/technologies.'

'Another interest was to use "light" in varied ways: transparent, translucent, opaque, shadow, and even a literal reference to the "kleeg light" that you see in the night skies in Los Angeles when there are premières of new movies and other events in the entertainment business.'

'Finally, the symbol for Lux Pictures re-emerges and becomes a sign-off on this loop and their corporate image again.' April Greiman.

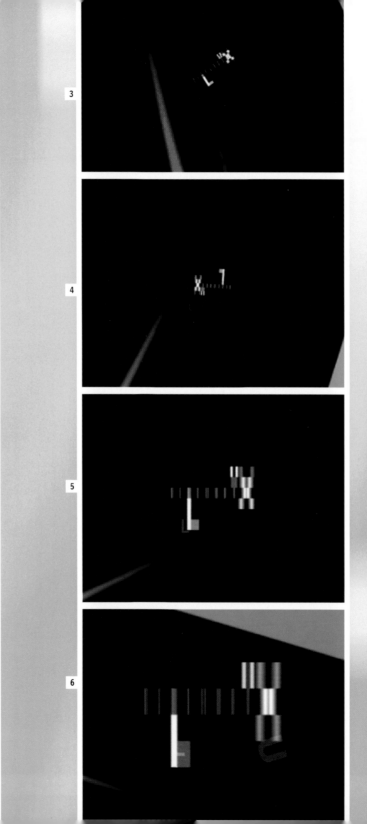

'THIS VERSION IS QUITE PRIMITIVE. IT'S MY FIRST ATTEMPT AT ADOBE AFTER EFFECTS AND IT'LL BE USED AS A FLICK-BOOK OPENING FOR THE LUX WEB SITE, AND A MORE DIMENSIONAL ONE WILL BE USED AS ONE OF THEIR OPENING TITLES. THIS IS JUST A SKETCH.'

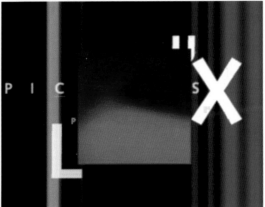

SOFTWARE/HARDWARE

PHOTOSHOP
ILLUSTRATOR
PAGEMAKER
AFTER EFFECTS

35MM CAMERA
POLAROID CAMERA
8MM VIDEO CAMERA
9500 AND 8500 POWERMACS

WORKING PROCESS

'I DO MOST OF THE SKETCHING IN MY HEAD IMMEDIATELY
AND START VISUALIZING ON THE COMPUTER. ONCE I HAVE
A GOOD IDEA IN MY MIND'S EYE I GO STRAIGHT TO THE
COMPUTER. TYPICALLY, THAT'S HOW IT HAPPENS.'
APRIL GREIMAN.

GREIMANSKI LABS
APRIL GREIMAN • 620 MOULTON AVENUE
SUITE 211 • LOS ANGELES • CA 90031 • USA

CLIENTS INCLUDE: California Institute of Architecture;
US West; Coop Himmelblau; Icon Shoes Corporation.
[SEE PAGE 149]

5. WORDS + PICTURES
FOR BUSINESS + CULTURE
***SWEATER* MAGAZINE**

LIFE **after** DARK

HOWIE B. ON U2 PAGAN FASHION ROCKERS HI-FI

DAFT PUNK

SWEATER

ISSUE 1 MAY 97
GRAB THIS SWEATER
PRINTED IN AMERICA

PROJECT CREDITS:

PUBLISHER: MARVIN SCOTT JARETT, PRESIDENT OF RAYGUN PUBLISHING
DESIGN DIRECTION: WORDS + PICTURES FOR BUSINESS + CULTURE:
P. SCOTT MAKELA AND LAURIE HAYCOCK MAKELA
ART DIRECTION: AMANDA SISSIONS
DESIGNERS: BRAD BARTLETT AND SUMMER POWER,
CRANBROOK ACADEMY OF ART GRADUATE STUDENTS

COMPANY BACKGROUND:

P. Scott and Laurie Haycock Makela are the co-chairpersons of 2-D design at Cranbrook Academy of Art. Laurie Haycock Makela was the design director of the Walker Art Center in Minneapolis, responsible for its graphic identity and designing exhibition catalogues. P. Scott Makela, director of Words + Pictures for Business + Culture, creates digital imagery and typography for print and film, including music videos for Miles Davis and more recently for Michael Jackson's ScreaM. In collaboration, they have produced film and video work for MCI, Prudential, Lotus Software and Warner Bros Records.

Amanda Sissions, the art director on *Sweater*, has worked with design group Substance, designing *Blah Blah Blah* (another RayGun publishing title), and projects for MTV and Warner Bros Music.

'LONG AFTER THE REST OF AMERICA HAS GONE TO SLEEP, AN IMPORTANT SUBCULTURE OF MUSICAL, ARTISTIC AND FASHIONABLE INNOVATIONS IS THRIVING INTO THE EARLY DAWN.' MARVIN SCOTT JARETT, PRESIDENT OF RAYGUN PUBLISHING.

KIND
OF
BLUE

Sweater is the latest magazine from Marvin Scott Jarett, publisher of *RayGun*, *Bikini* and *Blah Blah Blah*. *Sweater* is a bimonthly, 82 page, full-colour magazine focusing on

THE BRIEF: youth-culture nightlife across America. The magazine is distributed free at clubs, colleges and coffee houses and includes listings from all over the country.

As with the previous RayGun publishing titles, the look and design of *Sweater* had to say as much about its subject as the magazine's actual content. As the design directors on the project, P. Scott and Laurie Haycock Makela say:

'The pressure and exhilarating challenge of making graphic innovations in the "look" of subculture, edge, hip, new, more radical than rave, and urgent raw energy was compounded by a compressed time-line that gave us about two weeks to develop a logo, and about two weeks to put the interior together.'

After seeing Jaws at 11, he was hooked

ANIMAL FORM

Mod genius designer Paul Compitus likes to make clothes with fins and manes. Carol Leggett figures out why you would want to wear such things.

Left: Crochet gown by *PACO RABANE*. Camouflage & Fleece vest by *STUSSY*. Crochet blanket shawl by *MRS. MATTHEWS*.

The Bay City's notorious Hardkiss Bros. take Aidin Vaziri on a tour of their town. He lives to tell the tale.

SAN FRANC

Old School Electronica

By Jelene Hagelberg

LA promoter Philip Blaine has been responsible for some of the best clubs and concerts in Southern California. Plus, he likes fish. SWEATER contributor Nicole throws him a line

The Fisher King

T. Power, Junglist

We're calling this article "T. Power, Junglist" for the ironic entertainment value derived from the fact that the artist himself does not consider himself (strictly) a junglist, certainly, whatever that term might in fact mean anyway. Are we wrong? By Vivian Host.

DEVELOPING THE IDEA:

The project started with the magazine's title, *Sweater*, which came from Marvin Scott Jarett and the recruitment of an editor, Jim Greer. Jarett then approached P. Scott Makela and asked him to design a magazine 'cooler and cleaner than *RayGun*, *iD*, *Time Out* and the *Face*.' Words + Pictures was to develop the logo, cover and the 'vibe' for the magazine in collaboration with Amanda Sissions, who had just moved to Los Angeles from London to work full-time on *Sweater*.

The design process was incredibly intense with work happening on the project in Detroit, at Cranbrook Academy, and in Los Angeles over a few weeks. Hypothetical layouts and logo ideas were modemed and faxed from city to city with a final period of a week at the RayGun offices turning the basic design vocabulary into a working publication.

The design is based on HUD, a Words + Pictures house font in both vertical and horizontal configurations, contrasted with the classical face Bembo. P. Scott Makela describes the logo as 'neo-futuristic with a twist of Korean'.

thought

opportunity

SWEATER

PLEASURE

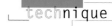

'In the case of Sweater, desktop technologies were valued mainly for transportation. For once, PhotoShop was not the dominant software. Quark and the WWW saved us because of all the files sent from coast to coast in minutes.'

SOFTWARE/HARDWARE

ILLUSTRATOR
FREEHAND
PHOTOSHOP
QUARKXPRESS
FONTOGRAPHER

POWERMACS

WORKING PROCESS

'WE HAD LIMITATIONS ON THE GYMNASTICS OF TYPOGRAPHY, THEREFORE WE HAD TO GO FOR THE EASY READ. IN THE LOGO FOR *SWEATER*, WE WANTED A HYBRID OF PACIFIC CYBERRIM AND US CULTURES. WE DESIGNED IT TO RUN VERTICALLY, BUT TO LOOK INTERESTING. IF YOU LOOK AT IT HORIZONTALLY, IT BEGINS TO LOOK LIKE FOREIGN/KOREAN CHARACTERS. THE CUSTOM TYPEFACE HUD HAS BEEN OUR HOUSE FONT FOR A WHILE AND WE HAVE FINALLY BEGUN TO IMPLEMENT IT INTO THE COMMERCIAL CULTURE.' P. SCOTT AND LAURIE HAYCOCK MAKELA.

WORDS + PICTURES FOR BUSINESS + CULTURE BOX 8384 • BLOOMFIELD HILLS MICHIGAN 48302. 8384 • USA

CLIENTS INCLUDE: MCI; Kodak; Nike; Ray Gun Publishing; American Photography; Warner Bros. Records; Prudential; Lotus Software; Propaganda Films.
[SEE PAGE 157]

6: VSA PARTNERS INC.
THE HARLEY-DAVIDSON WEB SITE

'THE PEOPLE WHO WE HOPE ARE VISITING THE HARLEY-DAVIDSON SITE ARE THE MOST IMPATIENT; THEY'RE PEOPLE WHO LIKE TO GET SOMEWHERE FAST AND IN STYLE. IN MANY WAYS IT'S AN "ANTI-WEB" SITE. WE WANT PEOPLE TO LOG ON, FIND THE INFORMATION THEY NEED AND GO AWAY AND START UP THEIR BIKES.'
GEOFF MARK, DIRECTOR OF NEW MEDIA AT VSA.

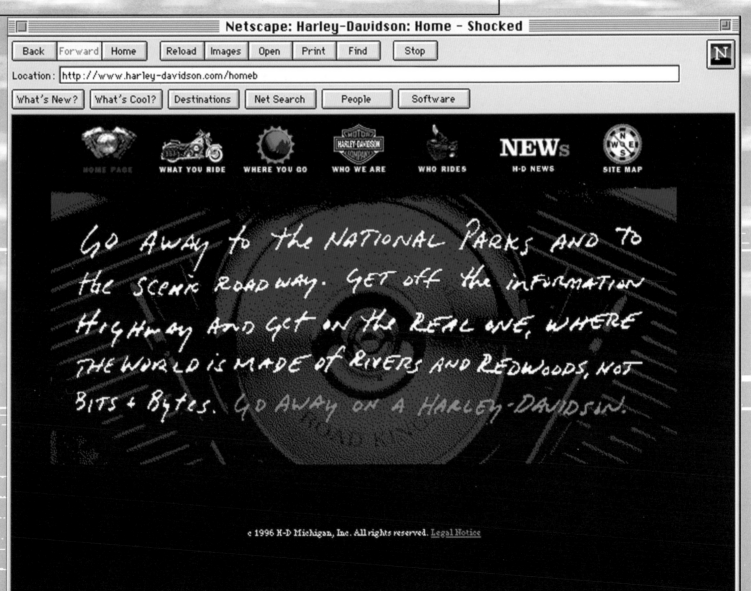

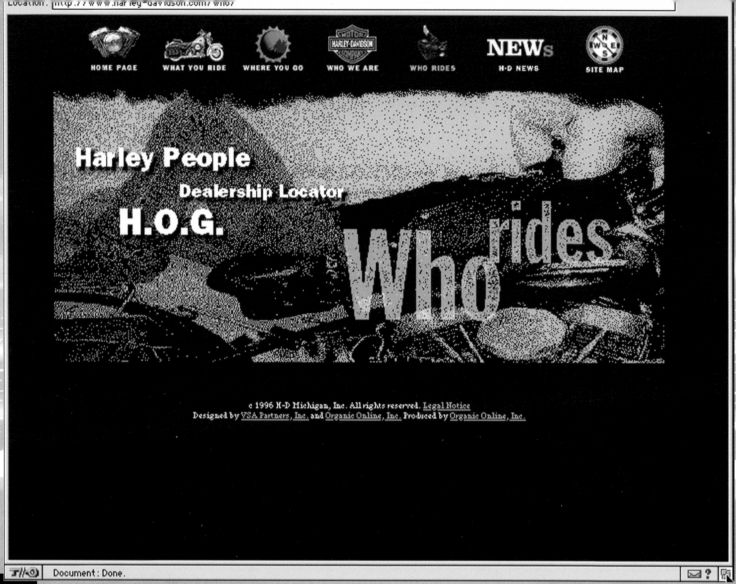

HOME PAGE WHAT YOU RIDE WHERE YOU GO WHO WE ARE WHO RIDES H-D NEWS SITE MAP

Harley People

Dealership Locator

H.O.G.

Who rides

Document: Done.

PROJECT CREDITS:

CREATIVE DIRECTORS:	DANA ARNETT
	CURT SCHREIBER
DESIGN DIRECTORS:	KEN FOX
	GEOFF MARK
DESIGNERS:	MIKE PETERSEN
	RON SPHON
WRITER:	JACK SICHTERMAN

COMPANY BACKGROUND:

VSA Partners in Chicago was formed in 1983 and is led by the firm's five partners: Robert Vogele, Dana Arnett, James Koval, Curtis Schreiber and Ken Schmidt. The firm ascribes its success to 'creative communications that are intelligent, non-traditional, emotional and effective'. It works with many of the world's most respected companies in strategic communication planning, corporate and brand identity, marketing and financial communications, film and multimedia productions.

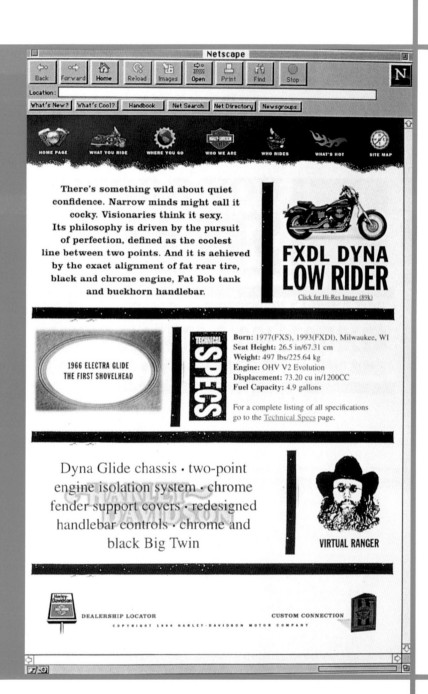

THE BRIEF:

Harley-Davidson is possibly the world's best known motorcycle company, avidly supported by millions of enthusiasts. The brief in building a Harley-Davidson World Wide Web site was to promote its brand identity as a global leader in the motorcycle industry while creating a demand for its products. The intention was to present information not only about the company's brand but also about events, people, the best places to ride and meet – ultimately, to make the site the premier motorcycling experience on the Web.

technique

As the potential of the Web is fully realized as a medium, it's easy for designers to get caught up in the technological aspect of the design to the detriment of the creative idea. Underlying the Harley-Davidson Web site is a coherent vision of the aims and objectives of the client and the clearest way of realizing them.

THE HOME PAGE ALLOWS THE USER TO CHOOSE BETWEEN AN ENHANCED, ANIMATED ROUTE INTO THE SITE WITH AUDIO OR, IF THEIR BROWSER ISN'T CAPABLE OF SUPPORTING SHOCKWAVE, A STANDARD VERSION. THE WORDING, IN THE SAME FORM AS THE HEALTH WARNING ON A CIGARETTE PACKET, IS IN KEEPING WITH HARLEY-DAVIDSON'S REBELLIOUS IMAGE.

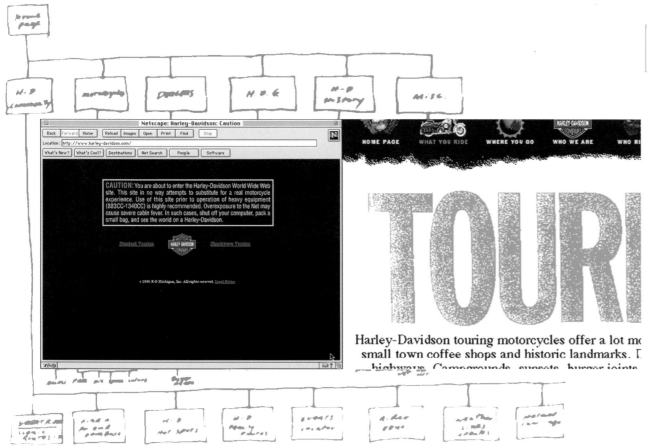

THE INITIAL APPROACH:

It was important that in presenting an established brand like Harley-Davidson with its own strong 'culture' the Web site fitted in with the overall feel of the company and its ethos. To this end, the initial stages of the design process involved close collaboration with the client in identifying and structuring content for the site while deciding on the overall style and tone of the site. To achieve this, VSA worked very closely with writer Jack Sichterman, a former Harley-Davidson employee, to summarise what that approach would be in the form of a mission statement:

'Throughout the 20th century, Harley-Davidson has been a leader in popular culture, to the extent that the motor company has become part of pop culture. It made sense that Harley-Davidson would not only participate in the growth of the World Wide Web, but take its rightful share in the development of it. As it influenced rock'n'roll in Hollywood, Harley's influence on the Web will be based on a grass-roots, covert movement based on look, feel, tone and attitude.'

'In the 1990s, people have left their televisions and magazines behind, not for the sporting life, but for the small screens of their computers and the Internet. While opening new channels of communication, the Net is also closing people into their homes and offices. It appears to be time for someone to remind the world that this planet is best experienced by "just doing it" rather than just watching it. Harley-Davidson is the perfect company to send that message. The tone of the Harley-Davidson site should be action-orientated: "Get away from your computer and go see the world." '

The intention from the beginning was to develop this idea of the 'anti-web' site, presenting the content as a tool for users to get the information they needed, log off and start up their bikes.

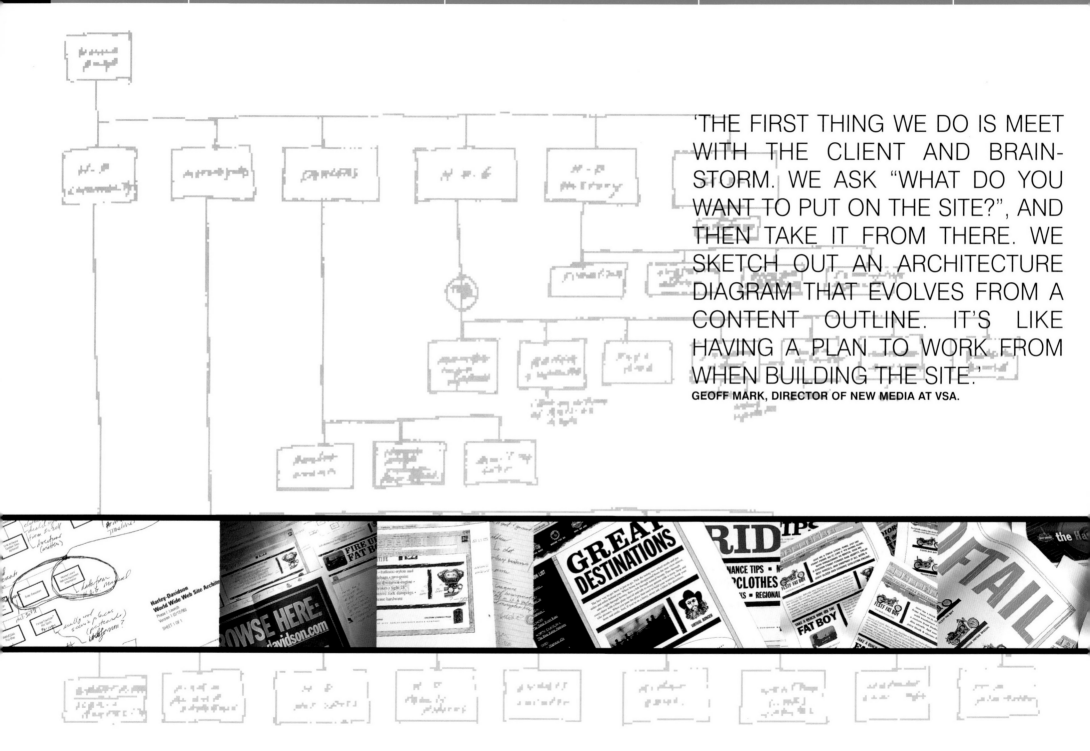

'THE FIRST THING WE DO IS MEET WITH THE CLIENT AND BRAINSTORM. WE ASK "WHAT DO YOU WANT TO PUT ON THE SITE?", AND THEN TAKE IT FROM THERE. WE SKETCH OUT AN ARCHITECTURE DIAGRAM THAT EVOLVES FROM A CONTENT OUTLINE. IT'S LIKE HAVING A PLAN TO WORK FROM WHEN BUILDING THE SITE.'

GEOFF MARK, DIRECTOR OF NEW MEDIA AT VSA.

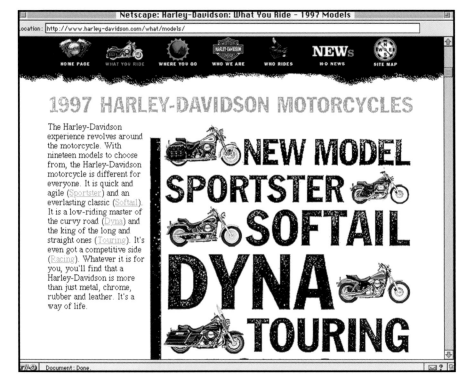

The structure and site architecture were mapped out on paper in graphic diagrammatic form. This was flexible so that it could evolve throughout the design process. Once the client had approved the architecture the focus shifted on to developing the look and feel of the site. Initial concepts and designs were worked up on Macintoshes using QuarkXPress and presented for approval.

With the client's consent, VSA moved on to produce the final animations, typographic and graphic imagery using Photo-Shop, GIFBuilder., screen captures and Debabelizer. The elements for the site were then forwarded to Organic Online in San Francisco for HTML programming. Designs were constantly reviewed online between the client in Milwaukee and VSA in Chicago while the designs actually 'resided' on a server in San Francisco.

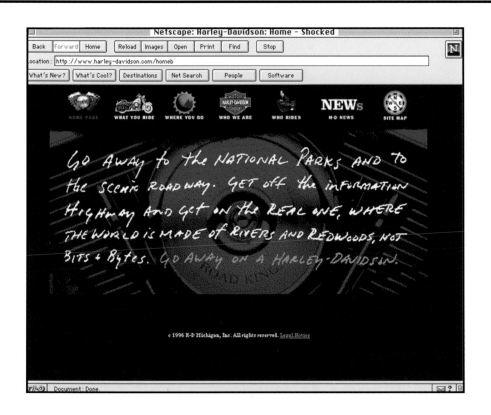

1

Visually the style of the site is bold and brash with a gritty, 'garage' type of feel. This is enhanced by the use of a carefully chosen limited colour palette which has the added benefit of smaller file sizes giving faster download times.

2

The second screen encourages the user to 'get off the Information Highway and get on the real one, where the world is made of rivers and redwoods, not bits and bytes'.

DESIGN AND TECHNOLOGY:

Designing online content for delivery over the Internet always involves a balance between the capabilities of technology and designing within those limitations. Larger, more complex graphics files take longer to download using the modem standard, 28.8 kbps. The Harley site had to be bold and brash in keeping with the company's image and also carry enough imagery to keep the users interested. The solution to this problem was to limit the colour palette to two or three colours for the large section menus and backgrounds. This meant that images could be full-screen but also worked well in creating the gritty, 'garage' feel of the graphics and typography. In this case, the limitations of the technology were vital in influencing the design of the site. The opening page of the site allows the user to choose between an animated home page or a faster still image, depending on the speed of their Internet access and the capability of their browser.

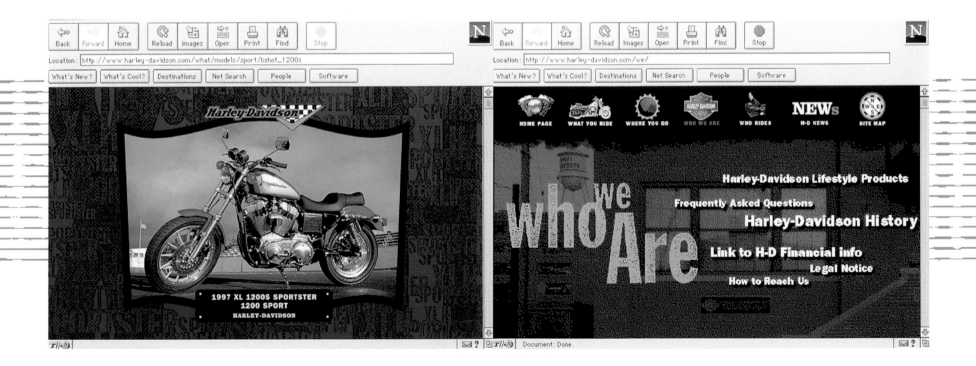

THE INTENTION FROM THE BEGINNING WAS TO DEVELOP THIS IDEA OF THE 'ANTI-WEB' SITE, PRESENTING THE CONTENT AS A TOOL FOR USERS TO GET THE INFORMATION THEY NEEDED, LOG OFF AND START UP THEIR BIKES.

SOFTWARE/HARDWARE

ILLUSTRATOR
PHOTOSHOP
PREMIERE
QUARKXPRESS
DEBABELIZER
DIRECTOR
SOUNDEDIT
NAVIGATOR

FETCH (FOR FTP)
EUDORA (FOR EMAIL)
POWERPC WORKSTATIONS
ARCUS II SCANNER

WORKING PROCESS

INITIAL PAPER LAYOUTS WERE PRODUCED USING QUARKXPRESS, ADOBE PHOTOSHOP AND ADOBE ILLUSTRATOR. ONCE THESE WERE APPROVED BY THE CLIENT THE FINAL GRAPHICS FOR THE SITE WERE CONVERTED INTO JPEG AND GIF FORMATS, THE STANDARD PICTURE FORMATS USED ON THE WORLD WIDE WEB. THE HTML CODING TO CONTROL THE LAYOUTS OF THE PAGES WAS CARRIED OUT BY SAN FRANCISCO-BASED

ORGANIC ONLINE, AND THE WORK IN PROGRESS WAS REVIEWED BY THE DESIGNERS AND CLIENT OVER THE INTERNET. ONE OF THE RECENT DEVELOPMENTS ON THE WORLD WIDE WEB IS THE ABILITY TO USE AUDIO AND VIDEO ELEMENTS ON A SITE, AS WELL AS ANIMATION. GIFBUILDER ALLOWS A SERIES OF STILL FRAMES TO BE COMPILED AND DELIVERED IN THE FORM OF A SIMPLE ANIMATION (ANIMATED BUTTON ON INDEX TOOLBAR).

VSA PARTNERS INC.
542 SOUTH DEARBORN • SUITE 202
CHICAGO • ILLINOIS 60605 • USA
CLIENTS INCLUDE: Aetna, Inc.; Capitol Records; The Coca-Cola Co.; Einstein Bros. Bagel Co.; Eastman Kodak Co.; General Motors Corp.; Nortel-Northern Telecom; Warner Bros; Time Warner, Inc.; Potlatch Corp..
[SEE PAGE 155]

7. JOHNSON BANKS
THE NATIONAL FILM AND TELEVISION SCHOOL

KEEP TECHNICAL AND CREATIVE

BRILLIANCE FLOWING

INTO THE INDUSTRY

PROJECT CREDITS:

DESIGN DIRECTOR: MICHAEL JOHNSON
DESIGNERS: MICHAEL JOHNSON, LUKE GIFFORD, HARRIET DEVOY
PHOTOGRAPHER: MARTIN BARRAUD
PRINTER: LITHOTECH

Johnson Banks was set up in 1992 by Michael Johnson. The original impetus for the company's formation was the belief that design could be both strategically correct and creatively excellent. Although the company only numbers six people in all, their clients range from blue-chip companies such as British Telecom to what Johnson describes as 'dream' clients such as The Royal Opera House and The Victoria and Albert Museum in London.

THE BRIEF:

The National Film and Television School (NFTS) in the United Kingdom was set up in 1971 and enjoys a worldwide reputation as a centre of excellence. While it has an impressive list of ex-students and sponsors inside and outside the industry, its visual identity was in 'desperate need of some graphic help', as Michael Johnson, design director on the project, thoughtfully puts it. 'They had a very traditional and small logo for the school, and supporting literature that was clean and minimal, but which hardly communicated the scope and fame of the place.' Johnson Banks was initially briefed by the client to look at the current literature, taking as its starting point the 1997 prospectus. As it happened, the company redesigned the whole way the school presents itself in all aspects of its corporate identity.

1

MICHAEL JOHNSON EXPLAINS THE PROBLEMS:

'IT WAS A COMPLEX BRIEF BECAUSE THEY NEEDED NOT JUST A LOGOTYPE OR SYMBOL FOR THE SCHOOL ITSELF, BUT ALSO A WAY TO LINK OTHER DIVISIONS SUCH AS CREATEC, THE NEW DIGITAL MEDIA AREA, TO THE SCHOOL. THE SCHOOL'S DIFFERENT DEPARTMENTS, LIKE EDITING AND ANIMATION, ALSO EXPRESSED A DESIRE TO HAVE THEIR OWN IMAGE.'

The previous logo for the school was simple, clean and minimal but, as Michael Johnson says, 'it hardly communicated the scope and fame of the school'. The new identity is much more than a stand-alone logotype and allows the school to brand and unify all the disparate areas it's involved in.

1
Starfish for the editing department.

2
A spread taken from the prospectus.

3
Back cover of the prospectus.

EACH YEAR BRINGS NEW TALENTS, NEW IDEAS NEW TECHNIQUES AND NEW TUTORS FROM THE INDUSTRY TO THE NFTS. WE MAKE THE CONNECTIONS TO KEEP THE UK AT THE LEADING EDGE OF CHANGE

With each new release and upgrade there is less and less that the software cannot do. Similarly the latest fonts can appear everywhere for a few months only to disappear when their 15 minutes of fame are over. As Michael Johnson says, 'we'll probably look back at the 90s and laugh at the amount of "PhotoShopped" images. It'll look a bit like psychedelic type and the 60s.'

2

Roger Crittenden Editing

Maggie Ellis Screen Sound

William Fitzwater Fiction Direction

Stephen Frears Fiction Direction

Lynn Horsford Producing

Peter Howitt Producing

Ian Ross Fiction Direction

Peter Morton Screen Design

Walter Lassally Cinematography

Rebecca O'Brien Producing

LEARNING THROUGH EXPERIMENT MEANS TAKING RISKS PROGRESS MEANS EXPLORING NEW TERRAIN

THE NFTS PROVIDES EXPERIENCED GUIDES TO SUPPORT STUDENTS' VISION AND SPIRIT OF ADVENTURE

THE INITIAL APPROACH:

'We started very broadly,' explains Johnson, 'exploring a variety of different solutions. Some were very simple visual ideas that changed in execution for different parts of the organization, some were more complex. Distilling a problem down to a clear and simple solution is our driving force; people come to us to communicate, not to confuse. What emerged as the strongest course of action was a radical departure for the process of corporate identity. This was based around "projection" – the name of the Film School, or one of its departments, projected on to photographic symbols of the relevant subject. We experimented with things like projecting the word "editing" on to a cleaver. This became even more interesting when the type seemed to go in and out of focus on the objects, and when applied in the prospectus we could take complete sentences and project them on to almost anything we wanted.' Using Adobe PhotoShop these roughs were manipulated to layer the text over various images and then blurred in parts to simulate the effect of the changing points of focus that they were after.

'The designers overlaid the type on to different objects using Adobe PhotoShop to produce visuals to show to the client. This allowed them to simulate the blurring effect that physically projecting the type with a slide projector would have produced. At this stage the choice of objects ranged from the obvious such as the abacus for a producer, to the bizarre, a starfish.'

REJECTED IDEAS:

Johnson Banks initially presented a series of ideas to the client before agreeing on the chosen solution. An idea based around a series of screens was rejected because the designers ultimately felt it would be too limiting to the identity. Similarly the 'logo in motion' looked too odd and would have been difficult to apply convincingly. The most radical departure from the adopted solution was the 'eye within the square' which Johnson describes as 'a continuous line starting out as a square which becomes a mess and then an eye. The idea is to allude to "giving" someone vision or teaching them to see.'

DEVELOPING THE IDEA:

The client approved the projection idea and the approach so the designers carried out a test with photographer Martin Barraud. 'In the photography trial we physically projected type on to the objects to see what could be achieved, and while this tended to lose fine detail we liked the overall effect,' says Johnson.

As things turned out, at the next presentation, the client actually preferred the original mock-ups. To combine the style of the real projections with the style of the roughs, the objects were re-photographed on their own with the intention of combining the type later. This wasn't without its own problems, as Johnson explains: 'For the large, full-page shots for the prospectus, the photographic subjects had to be very dark so that the "projected" white type could illuminate them. It was the first time we've had to ask our photographer to deliberately underexpose.' In the final proofing stage, taking the digital files to press, it was discovered that in reproduction some of the images were getting too dark and the originals themselves had to be lightened.

'IN THE PHOTOGRAPHY TRIAL WE PHYSICALLY PROJECTED TYPE ON TO THE OBJECTS TO SEE WHAT COULD BE ACHIEVED, AND WHILE THIS TENDED TO LOSE FINE DETAIL, WE LIKED THE OVERALL EFFECT.'

THE FINISHED PROSPECTUS:

The finished prospectus combines full-page images and spreads alongside the smaller visual identities for the different departments and disciplines as part of the page layouts. Johnson explains the thinking behind the overall look and feel:

'We wanted it to look very contemporary, of the next century, not this one. The photos led the whole thing and because there was a lot of type on them we kept the body copy type very simple. People need to read this document and get important information out of it; it has to be easy to digest. For this reason we used the fonts Trade Gothic condensed and Adobe Garamond, keeping the type pages light, contrasting with the darkness and density of the picture pages.'

The next stage in implementing the new look for the School will be to apply the departmental symbols to the specific literature that they each produce. The prospectus was very much a test case of the designs that will now be applied across the board, including the annual report.

NFTS STUDENTS NEED ENERGY TO SUPPORT THEIR TALENT AND A BURNING DESIRE TO IMPROVE THEIR SKILLS PLUS FOCUS TO BRING THEIR CREATIVITY TO FRUITION

MANY HANDS MAKE LIGHT WORK COLLABORATION IS THE KEY TO ALL SUCCESSFUL FILM, TELEVISION AND VIDEO PRODUCTION THE CURRENT CONVERGENCE BETWEEN INFORMATION, ENTERTAINMENT AND THE DIGITAL DOMAIN MEANS EVEN GREATER EMPHASIS ON TEAM EFFORT AT EVERY STAGE OF THE PROCESS

DESIGN AND TECHNOLOGY:

'A few years ago, when we couldn't really use the machines, it slowed things down a lot,' says Johnson. 'There was a phase then where you did everything on computer and it all looked computerized. Now we've reached the stage where "designer and computer" equals something we would never have thought of conventionally. It's an exciting time, but we're keen that our work doesn't look computerized – there are too many people accepting pixels as good, but we don't like them. The fact that we started the Film School project on computer, tried it out photographically and then went back to the computer was just the way it worked out. We still wanted it to be done in the camera, but it was just too difficult that way.'

'I think the only drag with the machines is that you can date a piece of work from the advent of a particular program. We'll probably look back at the 90s and laugh at the amount of "PhotoShopped" images. It'll look a bit like psychedelic type and the 60s.'

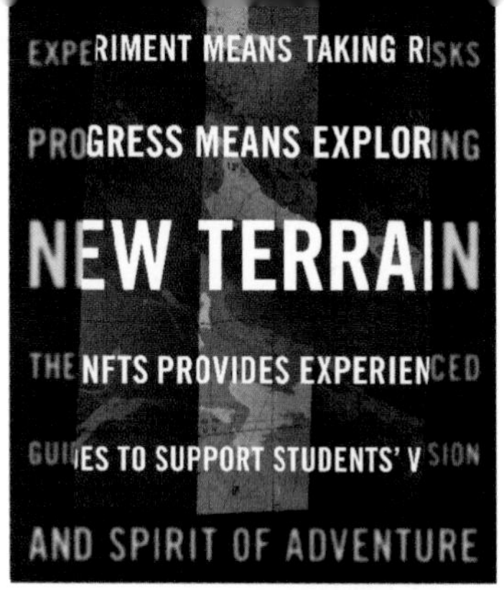

'The prospectus is "built" around the projected photographs. While these were very dense and heavy it was important to keep the information simple and easy to read on the text pages. For this reason there is a lot of white space. Extremely clear diagrams are used to give a quick overview of the three-year, full-time course outline. The fonts, Trade Gothic and Adobe Garamond, are renowned for their clarity and reader-friendliness.'

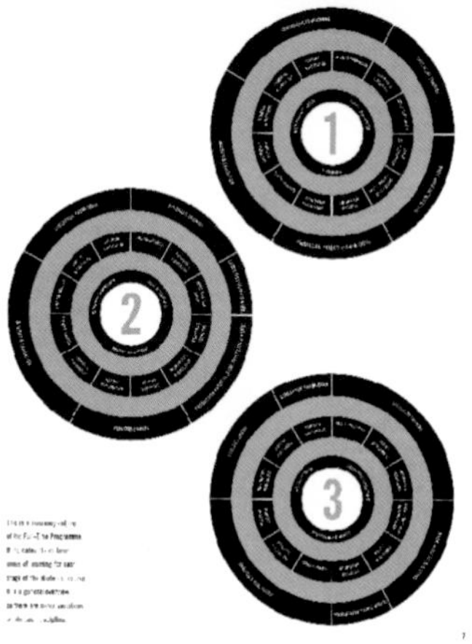

'WE WANTED IT TO LOOK VERY CONTEMPORARY, OF THE NEXT CENTURY, NOT THIS ONE. THE PHOTOS LED THE WHOLE THING AND BECAUSE THERE WAS A LOT OF TYPE ON THEM WE KEPT THE BODY COPY TYPE VERY SIMPLE.'

SOFTWARE/HARDWARE

FREEHAND
ILLUSTRATOR
QUARKXPRESS
PHOTOSHOP
POWERMACS

WORKING PROCESS

THE ORIGINAL VISUALS FOR THE IDENTITY FOR THE NATIONAL FILM AND TELEVISION SCHOOL WERE PUT TOGETHER USING FREEHAND, ILLUSTRATOR AND QUARKXPRESS ON THE MACINTOSH. THE PHOTOGRAPHIC IMAGES WERE HIGH-RESOLUTION DRUM-SCANNED AND PUT TOGETHER WITH THE TEXT IN PHOTOSHOP, WITH DUOTONES ADDED LATER. THE OVERALL LAYOUT OF THE PROSPECTUS HAS BEEN COMPILED IN QUARKXPRESS.

JOHNSON BANKS
STUDIO 6 • 92 LOTS ROAD • LONDON
SW10 0QD • UK

CLIENTS INCLUDE: British Telecom; The Victoria and Albert Museum; Polygram Records; the Red Cross.
[SEE PAGE 150]

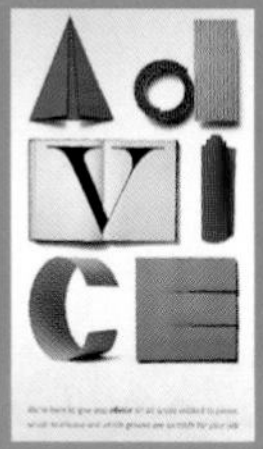

8. AUTOMATIC
IDENTITY FOR THE
PLAYGROUND MUSIC NETWORK

ELECTRIC KINGDOM

COMPANY BACKGROUND:

Automatic was formed in the summer of 1995 by Ben Tibbs and Martin Carty,
graphic design graduates from the Royal College of Art in London.

PROJECT CREDITS:

DESIGNERS

MARTIN CARTY
BEN TIBBS

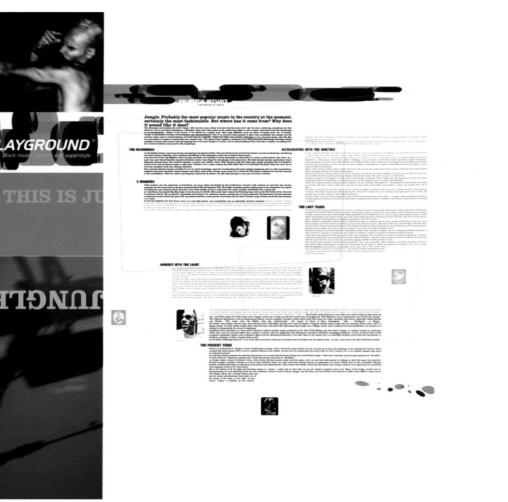

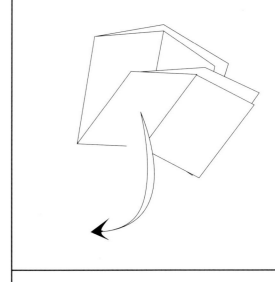

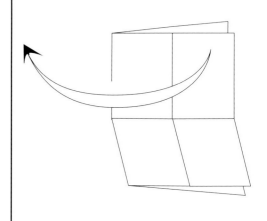

1

Automatic was approached by Equator International to develop the identity, structure and visual language for the newly-conceived Playground Music Network (PMN). This would be a 'specialist music and information service for those into black music, culture and style'. The concept – that Playground Music Network would be an interactive network allowing its users to exchange information about the music scene and industry – was well developed. However, how it

THE BRIEF:

would actually materialize was still to be decided. As a result the designers worked very closely with the client on the whole evolution and structure of the project alongside the design work. At this stage in the project it wasn't specified what form the Playground Music Network would take and whether it would be print- or screen-based.

1

'We sat down and talked, worked out the ideas and then took them to the computer to visualize them.'
The bulletin was always going to be a single sheet that folded out and the early discussion focused on a way of making that work. In the end, the designers settled on a multi-folded broadsheet arrangement where the whole thing would fold. The sheet is full-colour on one side and two colours on the other. When folded, the full-colour forms the front cover, the contents page on the back and the first editorial spread. Opening the next fold reveals the broadsheet-sized spread and a history of jungle music. Fully unfolding it brings the reader to the two-colour inner section and information on record labels, publishing and what's going on in the jungle scene at the moment. Clarendon is the main font used throughout for body text and much of the titling.

THE INITIAL APPROACH:

Early work on the project focused on developing the content for the Playground Music Network and how different elements could be integrated into the overriding concept – that it would be a network made up of smaller parts. The idea that emerged was to produce a bimonthly printed bulletin, Playground, alongside a regularly updated Web site, musicplayground.

The printed bulletin would focus on a different music genre – past, present and future – with interviews with artists, reviews of the music, news of events and feedback from readers.

The Web site would be the area where Playground members would communicate with each other directly through an interactive forum and also have access to, an expanded version of the printed bulletin with information on music technology, record companies and a real-time chat area.

The idea was that the stickers and the postcards were printed and delivered to the members as single, A4-perforated sheets. It added to the solidity of the pack that all the elements were based on the same paper size. Again, it reflects the idea of single parts forming a larger whole, whether as a member of a network, or the membership card as part of a larger sheet.

1

2

DEVELOPING THE IDEA:

'The themes we pushed evolved from the notion of a network – a complete whole created from many singular elements – which in this instance were its members, the black music and cultural genres that the Playground Music Network would explore and the areas, both print and onscreen, through which all the information would be channelled,' explains Martin Carty.

'These themes initially surfaced in the creation of the identity for the project. We'd originally decided it was important to connect the many disparate elements with a universal logo, but in the end, felt that the actual identity of Playground Music Network should be less static and more abstract than a simple logo would allow. This would be more representative of the diversity of the network. Taking abstract musical forms as the creative starting point, we gradually created a visual Playground theme tune – malleable and fluid enough to be sampled and reinvented for whatever direction the network takes.'

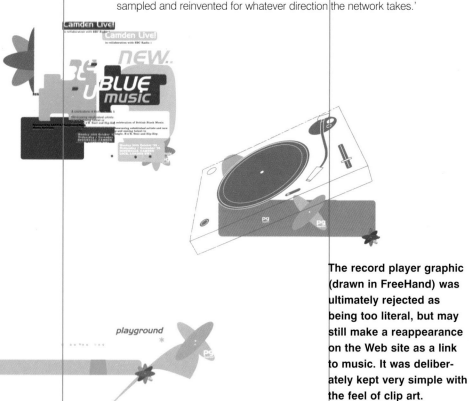

The record player graphic (drawn in FreeHand) was ultimately rejected as being too literal, but may still make a reappearance on the Web site as a link to music. It was deliberately kept very simple with the feel of clip art.

At the time the jungle bulletin was produced this was the only picture of 'Goldie' the designers had available. It's been heavily treated in PhotoShop to give it a feel more appropriate to the 'abstract organic' feel of the Playground Music Network identity.

pg ™
*musicplayground

The Web site for the Playground Music Network is currently under construction. It follows an easily navigable open structure and the primary intention is to have regularly updated news and information aimed at its members.

1

The jungle section opens with a graphic header outlining the areas available.

2

The site uses the same colour coding as the print edition of the bulletin, jungle is green and reggae is red.

3

The subsections continue the coding, each against a simple background. Despite the intensely graphic appearance of the pages, the file sizes are kept to a minimum by the careful use of a limited palette.

The page backgrounds are worked on as a series of layers before finally being flattened and saved in GIF format.

4

A home page splash opens – this automatically opens the 'real' home page which links to the different areas of the site through menu icons.

8.4

electronic workshop
automatic
identity for the playground music network
working process
074.075

'WE USED FREEHAND FOR ALMOST EVERYTHING INCLUDING TEXT LAYOUT. FREEHAND IS VERY INTUITIVE, YOU CAN LITERALLY DRAG COLOURS OFF PALETTES, IT'S ALMOST LIKE YOU CAN GET YOUR HANDS ON THE PAGE. THE TEXT FEATURE ON FREEHAND HAS GOT SO MUCH BETTER. IT'S NOT AS SYSTEMATIC AS QUARK, SO YOU'D USE THAT FOR A LONG DOCUMENT OR MAGAZINE, BUT YOU CAN ALWAYS DO THINGS IN FREEHAND AND BRING THEM IN.'

Ben Tibbs.

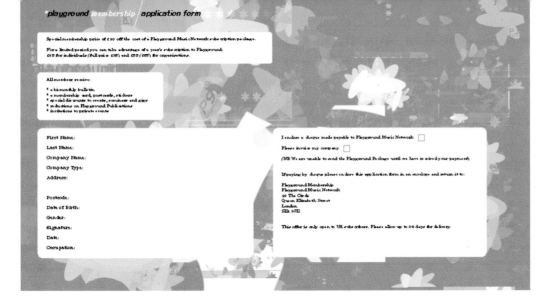

playground membership / **application form**

Special membership prices of £10 off the cost of a Playground Music Network subscription package.

For a limited period you can take advantage of a year's subscription to Playground: £35 for individuals (full price £35) and £55 (£65) for organisations.

All members receive:
* a bi-monthly bulletin
* a membership card, postcards, stickers
* special discounts to events, seminars and gigs
* reductions on Playground Publications
* invitations to private events

First Name:
Last Name:
Company Name:
Company Type:
Address:

Postcode:
Date of Birth:
Gender:
Signature:
Date:
Occupation:

I enclose a cheque made payable to Playground Music Network ☐

Please invoice my company ☐

(NB We are unable to send the Playground Package until we have received your payment)

If paying by cheque please enclose this application form in an envelope and return it to:

Playground Membership
Playground Music Network
10 The Circle
Queen Elizabeth Street
London
SE1 2JE

This offer is only open to UK subscribers. Please allow up to 20 days for delivery.

The identity for Playground successfully carries the identity across different media (here print), creating a fluid and coherent brand experience.

The development of the Music Playground Network identity involved creating something that would work in different media and situations, while still referring to the Network as a single entity. Key elements that give the identity its strength are used to brand it regardless of whether it's appearing in print or onscreen.

SOFTWARE/HARDWARE

FREEHAND
PHOTOSHOP
POWERMACS

WORKING PROCESS

'THE IMAGES ARE WORKED ON IN FREEHAND AND TAKEN INTO PHOTOSHOP WHERE THERE'S A LOT MORE TEXTURE AND DEPTH. OFTEN THEY ARE THEN TAKEN BACK TO FREEHAND, PLAYED AROUND WITH AND TAKEN BACK INTO PHOTOSHOP. ULTIMATELY, IT'S A MORE PAINTERLY APPROACH AND YOU FEEL THAT YOU'VE GOT YOUR HANDS ON THE ACTUAL ARTWORK RATHER THAN SITTING AT A COMPUTER.'
BEN TIBBS.

AUTOMATIC
15 IRVING STREET • LEICESTER SQUARE
LONDON • WC2H 7AU • UK

CLIENTS INCLUDE: MTV Europe; Ogilvy & Mather; Roose & Partners; Warner Music; nu-media research; Routlegde; Cartlidge Levene; Syzygy; Tinderbox; Bob Baxter/Amalgam and Equator International. **[SEE PAGE 146]**

9. AMXDIGITAL
BRITISH DESIGN AND ART DIRECTION CD-ROM

Michael Bierut Pentagram New York
Peter Carrow The Partners
Susanna Cucco Bianco & Cucco
Laura Heard CDT Design
Anthony Michael Michael Nash Associates
Quentin Newark Atelier
Pierre Vermeir HGV

3 of 3   more

PROJECT CREDITS:

DESIGNED
AND PRODUCED BY: AMXdigital

DESIGN DIRECTOR: Malcolm Garrett
INTERACTIVE DIRECTOR: Alasdair Scott
SENIOR DESIGNER: David Loosmore
DESIGNERS: Barrie Stjon Jones
                                                    Cara Mannion
PRODUCTION MANAGER: Zoe Black

Sponsored by Apple
Computer [UK] Ltd.
project manager for D&AD
Kathryn Patten

COMPANY BACKGROUND:

Formed in 1994 by Malcolm Garrett and Alasdair Scott, AMXdigital is a multimedia production and publishing company. Although its core interests are in the Internet and CD-ROM, it is also involved in the newer technologies such as Interactive TV, Video On Demand and multimedia databases. The company is based in London with an agent representing it in Tokyo.

'WE WANTED TO USE THE CONCEPT OF AN "INTELLIGENT BOOK" – IN OTHER WORDS, A PAGE-BASED METAPHOR USING "HYPERTEXT" TO ALLOW SWIFT NAVIGATION. WE'VE PROVIDED MENUS ON EVERY PAGE SO THAT USERS CAN QUICKLY JUMP FROM ONE SECTION TO ANOTHER AND WITH VERY FEW ANIMATED LINKS. ANIMATION IS WAY-COOL FOR SOME USES, BUT WE FIGURE THAT AFTER FOUR MONTHS OF USE, ANIMATED LINKS WITHIN A REFERENCE WORK SUCH AS THE D&AD CD-ROM BECOME EXTREMELY TEDIOUS.'
ALASDAIR SCOTT, AMXDIGITAL.

Founded in 1962, British Design and Art Direction (D&AD) is a professional association working on behalf of the design and advertising communities. D&AD is best known for its annual awards scheme which in 1996 received over 14,000 entries from around the world. From the awards, D&AD produces an annual of over 500 pages showcasing that year's winners.

'The brief was actually quite straightforward. We were asked to put everything that's in the D&AD print annual on the CD-ROM, so that everything that is meant to move, moves,' says Malcolm Garrett. 'The annual includes a lot of audio and video material that you just can't do justice to on paper.'

THE BRIEF:

THE INITIAL APPROACH:

'It was a ridiculously short turnaround. On the positive side, we were very clear on what the content was going to be as essentially it would be the same as the print annual,' explains Malcolm Garrett. 'The main problem was that the material that would have to go on the CD-ROM had been collected solely with the intention of using it in print. The text was more or less ready but all the images, video and audio had to be reconfigured specifically for digital publication.' Work started in July 1996 with a provisional deadline for the end of September that same year. 'By this time we had a running version (off a hard drive) with all the guts of the project in place. It was good to have a tight deadline because it pushed us to get it done. That version incorporated the final style, layout and structure with only a few missing sections,' says Garrett.

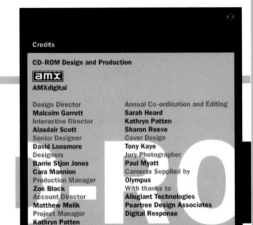

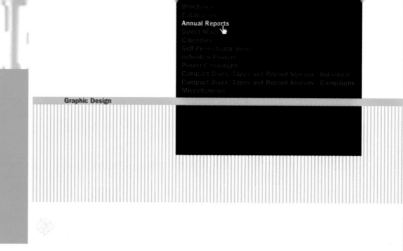

Graphic Design

Television and Cinema Advertising Crafts Direction

Please insert CD 1

more ▶] [◀ search ▶]

Sponsored by Tony Kaye Films

DEVELOPING THE IDEA:

'The main intention with the design was to make the navigation "invisible", so what we did was always subservient to the content, which is a diverse range of material and of course the most important thing about the CD. At the same time we didn't want to make it so plain that it'd appear bland,' explains Garrett.

Similarly because of the huge amount of information that needed to be included, the awards needed to be split across four CDs.
'Our intention was to make the transition between CDs as seamless as possible. The way we solved it was by putting everything except the video on every CD. We also felt it was important to get all the winning video on to disk one, the installation disk, so that if you only wanted to look at the major award winners there would be no disk swapping at all. Even so, the computer intelligently knows which disk is in the drive at any time, so it always knows what it has access to and which disk to point you to.'

THE DESIGN PROCESS:

Due to the fast turnaround needed on this job, a number of things were dealt with simultaneously:

- **general structure and how different elements linked together**
- **the interface styling**
- **the video compression to fit the huge amount of data into the available space**
- **compiling and cleaning up the database**

STRUCTURE AND INTERFACE:

'In retrospect it all seems pretty straightforward. The major section was the awards themselves, getting the navigational structure right because that was crucial and dictated the structuring of the other sections.'

The main screen, after the copyright preamble whilst the CD loads, takes the user straight to a menu for the main five sections:

- **about the CD**
- **about the awards**
- **about the D&AD**
- **searching for specific awards**
- **the sponsors**

Rolling over with the mouse highlights each of the sections in D&AD's corporate colours. This was actually one of the last screens to be designed.

Clicking on any of the five options takes the user to that area with further options for the Sub-categories in that area. At the same time it is possible to get back to any earlier section using the pop-up menus in the bottom left-hand corner of the screen.

In each of the awards categories the winners are listed in a roll-over menu and clicking on them reveals an enlarged picture of the work.

'We decided on a clean, white interface, not dissimilar to the pages of a book which of course it relates to,' explains Malcolm Garrett. 'You navigate using the onscreen menus. We went for a development of the Macintosh menu style. When the Mac's menu options are available they're black, and when they're not they're greyed out. In ours, when the options are available they're grey, and when they're not available they're simply not visible.'

Sponsored by James McNaughton Paper Group

Television and Cinema Advertising Crafts Direction
Accepted Abbott Mead Vickers. BBDO

Twister
Volvo Car UK Ltd

Television and Cinema Advertising Crafts Direction
Accepted Abbott Mead Vickers. BBDO

Twister
Volvo Car UK Ltd

more   search

Sponsored by Tony Kaye Films

CD-ROM
D&AD
Awards
Search

Exit

THE DATABASE:

The most important feature of this CD-ROM is the huge database of information about each entrant. Using the database to structure the content means that it can be searched or browsed in whatever way the user wants. At each stage there are a series of choices so that the relevant section of information can be reached easily and quickly.

Each winner has at least five pieces of data corresponding to them:
- **the title of the work**
- **an agency or design group**
- **an award**
- **a category**
- **a sub-category**

In addition, there is a certain amount of other possible data attached to it such as the complete list of credits and the jury. Selecting an entry means that the database calls up all the relevant information.

'One way of looking at it is that here's a bunch of things you might want to look at in a variety of ways and what we've done is built a front-end navigational system that will allow you to talk to that database in a seamless way so you don't even notice what's going on in the background,' says Malcolm Garrett.

The 'Search' section works by category or award, or in the way that the people in the book are categorized – editors, art directors and so on. It is possible to double up the search criteria to find award-winning art directors, for example. The search results take you directly to the found pieces in the context that they appear in the awards section. You can then step forwards or backwards through all the results you have found. The results stay highlighted even when the browser looks at something else until a new search is done. Whilst anomalies in a printed index go largely unnoticed, in a digital system any mistakes are completely obvious when it returns the wrong results. Thus, a large proportion of the time on a job like this is tracking down and eliminating any inconsistencies.

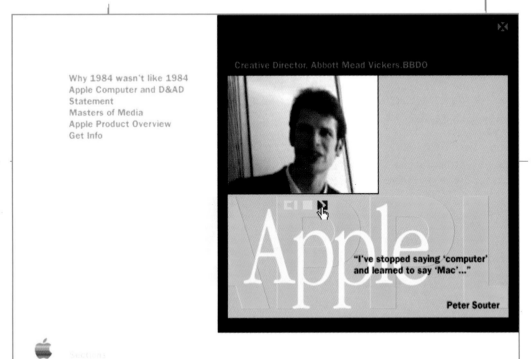

Why 1984 wasn't like 1984
Apple Computer and D&AD
Statement
Masters of Media
Apple Product Overview
Get Info

Creative Director, Abbott Mead Vickers.BBDO

Apple

"I've stopped saying 'computer' and learned to say 'Mac'..."

Peter Souter

HARDWARE AND SOFTWARE:

AMXdigital chose to use SuperCard for the project, rather than Macromedia Director, as the primary function of each CD-ROM is to provide fast, flexible access to a wealth of information rather than an interactive-rich environment.

'We use SuperCard for data-rich Macintosh-only CD-ROM development. SuperCard's multi-window support, combined with powerful scripting, extensibility via a plug-in architecture and the ability to build its content on-the-fly provided the most flexible authoring environment,' says Alasdair Scott.

technique

The D&AD CD-ROM is intended as a reference tool and from that point of view the most important element is the information it contains. To that end, the 'design' element of the project focuses on making the access and manipulation of that information as quick and flexible as possible.

'There is over three hours of video content across four CD-ROMs. When we came to film the interviews and the Apple testimonial sections we were conscious that these clips would be seen alongside multimillion pound advertising commercials. Rather than try to compete visually, we just went out with a Hi-8 and shot some footage. What was being said in the interviews was intrinsically more important than how it was said.'

'ALL THE MULTIMEDIA ELEMENTS RUN UNDER APPLE'S QUICKTIME MEDIA LAYER WHICH PROVIDES AN EXTREMELY POWERFUL, DYNAMIC MEDIA FORMAT. SUPERCARD OFFERS RIDICULOUSLY PRECISE CONTROL OF QUICKTIME, ALLOWING US TO DESIGN AN INTERFACE THAT WORKED THE WAY WE WANTED TO, NOT THE WAY THE OPERATING SYSTEM WANTED TO.'

The information on the CD-ROM is structured around a series of pop-up menus and roll-over menus. The result is that navigation from one section, or even subsection, is easy and intuitive with the least possible amount of 'clicking'.

Brand Identity
Title Sequences
Television Sponsorship Credits

Television and Cinema Graphics

SOFTWARE/HARDWARE

HI-8
PREMIERE
BETASP
QUICKTIME MEDIA LAYER

POWERMACS
DEBABELISER
ILLUSTRATOR
SUPERCARD

WORKING PROCESS

'ALL THE VIDEO WAS DIGITIZED FROM BETASP ON TO APPLE MACINTOSH USING ADOBE PREMIERE. WE USED SOME IN-HOUSE TRICKS TO GET THE VERY BEST VIDEO QUALITY AND EACH CLIP WAS ANALYSED SEPARATELY TO PROVIDE THE VERY BEST PLAYBACK QUALITY. WE OPTED FOR 25 FRAMES PER SECOND SINCE A LOT OF THE MATERIAL HAD FAST EDITS WHICH WOULD BE LOST WITH A LOWER FRAME RATE AND THIS MEANT THERE WERE SEVERAL LATE NIGHTS OF COMPRESSION. LUCKILY WE HAD SIX POWER MACINTOSHES ON CALL TO CRUNCH THE NUMBERS.'

AMXDIGITAL
VICTORIA HOUSE • 64 PAUL STREET
LONDON • EC2A 4NA • UK

CLIENTS INCLUDE: CompuServe; Warner Music; Saatchi & Saatchi; Ogilvy & Mather; Lowe Howard-Spink; Paramount Pictures. **[SEE PAGE 144]**

10. PAULA SCHER, PENTAGRAM NY
THE PUBLIC THEATER IDENTITY AND ADVERTISING

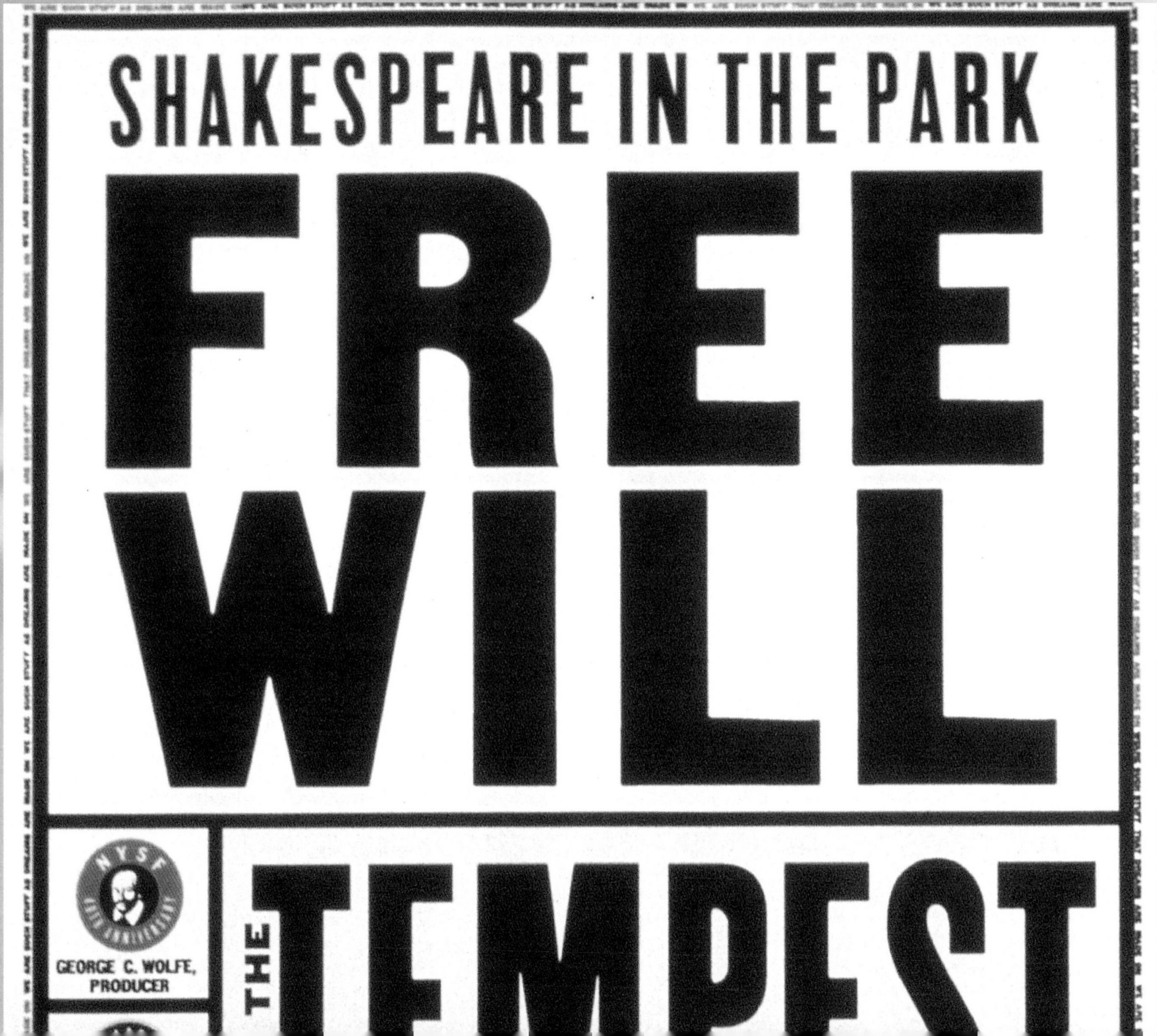

COMPANY BACKGROUND:

Pentagram is an international design partnership founded in 1972 with offices in New York, London, San Francisco, and Austin. The firm provides services in graphic, product and environmental design. There are 14 partner-principals and over 140 staff members worldwide. Each partner has areas of expertise in graphics, industrial design or architecture, and all have professional connections within the design, arts and academic communities.

Paula Scher began her career in the '70s as a record cover art director at both Atlantic and CBS Records. She founded her own firm with partner Terry Koppel in the '80s, then joined Pentagram as a partner in 1991.

SHAKESPEARE IN THE PARK
FREE WILL

NYSF

GEORGE C. WOLFE, PRODUCER

THE TEMPEST

ENTRANCES: CENTRAL PARK WEST
AT 81ST ST & 5TH AVE AT 79TH ST
CALL 212 861 7277 OR
212 598 7500 FOR DETAILS

DIRECTED BY GEORGE C. WOLFE   JUNE 22 – JULY 19

TROILUS & CRESSIDA

AUGUST 4 – SEPTEMBER 3 · DIRECTED BY MARK WING-DAVEY

MAJOR SUPPORTERS: TDI · WCBS NEWSRADIO 88 · NYNEX · New York Newsday

THE PUBLIC THEATER

THE JOSEPH PAPP PUBLIC THEATER

425 LAFAYETTE STREET

LIVE

For four decades, the New York Shakespeare Festival/Public Theater has brought the works of William Shakespeare free to the people of New York. Recent cuts in funding and shifting priorities jeopardize the Joseph Papp legacy of free Shakespeare for everyone. We are resolute in our commitment to preserving this important institution. Free Will.

Free Shakespeare in Central Park is presented with the cooperation of the City of New York. Rudolph W. Giuliani, Mayor. The City Council. Peter F. Vallone, Speaker. Schuyler Chapin, Commissioner, Department of Cultural Affairs. Henry J. Stern, Commissioner, Department of Parks and Recreation.

ADDITIONAL SUPPORT:

George Delacorte Fund

The Gladys Krieble Delmas Foundation

The Starr Foundation

Herman Goldman Foundation

The Eleanor Naylor Dana Charitable Trust

Helena Rubinstein Foundation

The Christian A. Johnson Endeavor Foundation

National Endowment for the Arts

New York State Council on the Arts

TUESDAY THROUGH SUNDAY EVENINGS AT

8 PM

TICKET POLICY

PICK UP YOUR FREE TICKETS ON THE DAY OF THE PERFORMANCE FROM 1 PM ON AT THE DELACORTE IN CENTRAL PARK OR 1-3 PM AT THE PUBLIC THEATER.

THE BRIEF:

The Public Theater in New York grew out of the New York Shakespeare Festival. Originally founded in 1954 by Joseph Papp, it was based on the belief that theatre of the highest quality should be available to everyone regardless of their culture, background or economic situation. The appointment of George C. Wolfe as producer in 1994 brought a renewed commitment to the ideals of its founder. With the intention of enlarging the scope and diversity of its audience, the Public, as it is known, would promote itself as streetwise, accessible and relevant to the non-theatre going public.

In fulfilling these aims, there were certain perception problems to overcome for the new producer. There was a confusion for many people between the New York Shakespeare Festival and the Public Theater, and also the smaller theatres within the main building, each with its own character. It was a question of an overall image of the venue and allowing the companies within it to maintain their own individuality.

THE INITIAL APPROACH:

The job wasn't simply a case of clearing up misunderstandings about the various elements of the theatre. The Public Theater had fallen into decline after its founder, Joseph Papp, died in 1991, and was still linked in most people's minds to the legendary producer. At this stage the theatre had little chance but to flounder. Thus the theatre's identity had to change out of absolute necessity.

George C. Wolfe came in as producer in 1994 and wanted to develop The Public into something vital, alive, young and broad; something for all the people of New York City. The identity had to be reinvigorated to communicate this new energy and direction, it had to announce something new was happening at The Public and change people's perceptions and misconceptions of what it was about.

DEVELOPING THE IDEA:

The initial design project Pentagram undertook for The Public Theater was the promotion of the summer 1994 New York Shakespeare Festival. 'Wives' and 'Kate' were shorthand for 'The Merry Wives of Windsor' and 'Kiss Me, Kate', Cole Porter's musical interpretation of 'The Taming of the Shrew'. 'Free! Live! No Waiting!' loudly announced a new ticket purchasing policy. The all-type approach was derived from early English theatre advertising, the expressions lifted from sidewalk barkers.

Just before opening night, representatives of Cole Porter's estate objected to altered dialogue in Wolfe's production of 'Kiss Me, Kate'. 'Kate' was cancelled and a back-up production of 'The Two Gentlemen of Verona' was put on in its place. The type-only treatment of the already-installed outdoor advertising permitted correction by 'snipping' – simply pasting the new information on to the original posters and billboards. 'Wives/Kate' became the semantically tidier 'Wives/Gents'.

The identity's visual language grew out of this happy accident. The typographic approach was broad, loud, from-the-hip, and left room for error, making it completely in the spirit of George Wolfe's approach to theatre and his vision of The Public as streetwise, timely, and accessible.

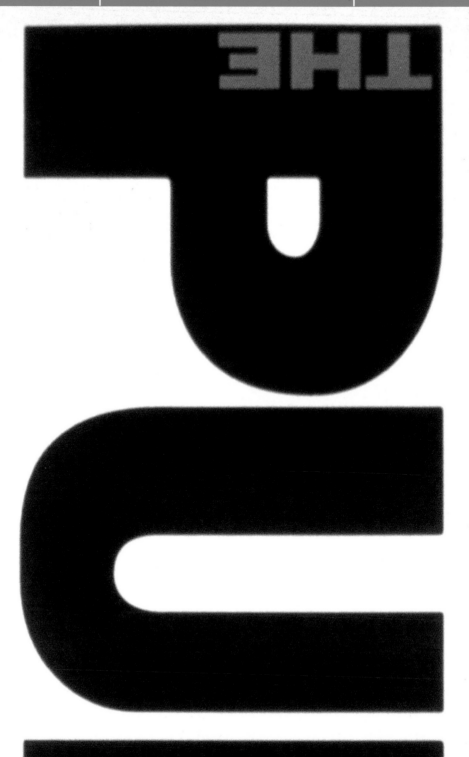

The success of the typographic approach established a direction for the institution's permanent graphic identity. The Public Theater logotype, a rectangular assemblage of woodcut typefaces, was designed to be the 'umbrella' or corporate logo. The boldness of the logo itself evokes a feeling of coming from the street while the design is subtle and flexible enough to be used in a variety of contexts. The emphasis on the word 'Public' is deliberate; it expresses Wolfe's inclusive vision for 'a theatre for the people'. It's also stacked on its side like a New York skyscraper.

A series of monogrammed roundels or stamps, recalling the NYC subway token, was designed to identify the different venues and activities within the institution as sub-brands of The Public.

PUBLIC
THEATER

425 LAFAYETTE STREET
(212) 260-2400

WRITTEN BY
STEVE MARTIN

DIRECTED BY
BARRY EDELSTEIN

WASP

PATTER FOR THE FLOATING LADY · THE ZIG-ZAG WOMAN

THE POSTERS:

When Joseph Papp was producer at The Public Theater, Paul Davis produced a memorable series of illustrated posters which set the standard for theatrical promotion for nearly a decade. Davis' play posters were established classics, painterly and moody. They were inextricably linked with Joe Papp's persona.

Pentagram's use of photos and Constructivist-inspired type represented a dramatic departure from the illustrations Paul Davis created during Joe Papp's tenure. As visually noisy as New York streets, the new look reflects Wolfe's outspoken attitude. The designs recall the hand-bills distributed in the street to promote anything from boxing to soap powder from earlier in the century. Certainly the inspiration comes from the street and its graphics, but it would be wrong to see them simply as copies as there is nothing else quite like them. While most theatre publicity still reflects a somewhat more genteel approach, Scher's work has been described as shouting with type. In this way the posters engage New Yorkers in a communal conversation with the theatre itself.

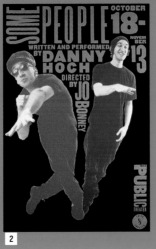

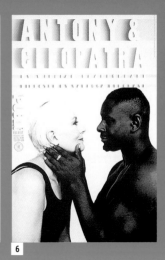

1. Him – December 1994.
2. Some People – October 1994.
3. Simpatico – November 1994.
4. Dancing On Her Knees – 1996.
5. Venus – March 1996.
6. Anthony & Cleopatra – January 1997.
7. Henry VI – October 1996. Shakespeare's epic in two parts, 'The Edged Sword' and 'Black Storm'.
8. The Diva Is Dismissed – October 1994. Jenifer Lewis's one-woman show.

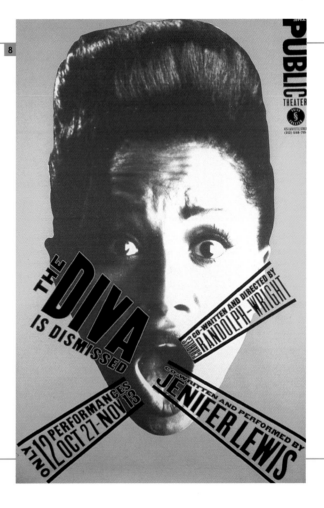

DESIGN AND TECHNOLOGY:
Paula Scher's typographic concepts are executed by her design team at Pentagram and the Public Theater's in-house designer, who complete the specific layouts.

'EVERYTHING IS DONE ON THE COMPUTER, AND I NEVER TOUCH IT. THE COMPUTER IS COMPLETELY IRRELEVANT TO ME, BUT IT IS RELEVANT TO GETTING THE WORK DONE.'
Paula Scher.

The identity for the Public reaches beyond a single logo and allows a huge range of applications in many different settings. The posters are designed with an awareness of the context and their use on the street, and much of their impact is gained by the way they contrast with what's alongside them.

Photographic Credits:
Peter Margonelli, Reven TC Wurman, Kurt Koepfle, Matt Petosa
Actor Portraits: Richard Avedon, Brigitte Lacombe, Michal Daniel, Carol Rosegg, Peter Harrison, Paula Court, Teresa Lizotte

SOFTWARE/HARDWARE

POWERMACS
ILLUSTRATOR
PHOTOSHOP

PENTAGRAM DESIGN INC.
204 FIFTH AVENUE • NEW YORK
NY 10010 • USA

CLIENTS INCLUDE: American Institute of Architects; Bausch & Lomb; Cirque du Soleil; Fuji; JP Morgan; Liz Claiborne; Phillips Van Heusen; Samsung; Texaco; United Airlines. [SEE PAGE 151]

origins · people · production · commercials · **fit guide**

11. ANTIROM
INTERACTIVE KIOSKS FOR THE LEVI'S STORES

COMPANY BACKGROUND:

Antirom grew out of a collective project to develop an alternative approach to the potential of CD-ROMs. Funded by the Arts Council of Great Britain the group produced the first Antirom CD-ROM at the start of 1995. Spurred on by the lack of imagination of previous employers in the interactive industry, the same members formed a limited company to 'develop experimental interactive strategies in a commercial sphere'. Coming from a diverse range of backgrounds in interactive media, from kiosks to Internet projects, the group's members believe that there isn't a single formula for success in interactive media and that each new project imposes unique design issues.

517 relaxed
Button Fly

Jeans for women
501
regular
Button Fly

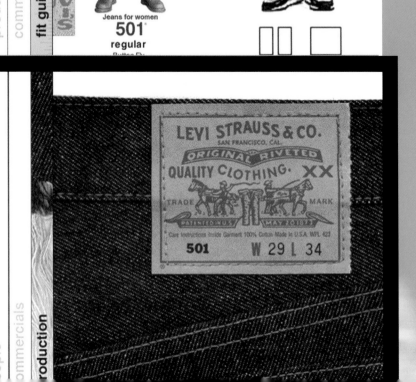

517
relaxed
Button Fly

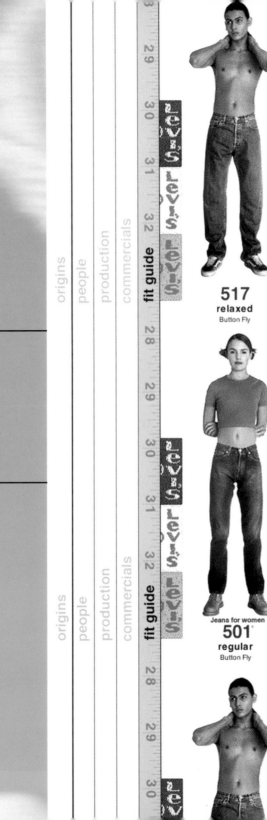

Jeans for women
501
regular
Button Fly

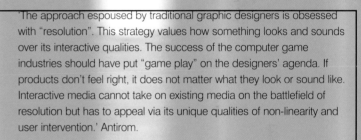

'The approach espoused by traditional graphic designers is obsessed with "resolution". This strategy values how something looks and sounds over its interactive qualities. The success of the computer game industries should have put "game play" on the designers' agenda. If products don't feel right, it does not matter what they look or sound like. Interactive media cannot take on existing media on the battlefield of resolution but has to appeal via its unique qualities of non-linearity and user intervention.' Antirom.

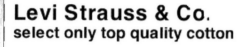

Levi Strauss & Co.
select only top quality cotton

Spinning

'WE DECIDED NOT TO FOLLOW THE "HOME PAGE" MODEL WHERE USERS NAVIGATED FROM A MAIN MENU DOWN INTO THE CONTENT, BUT CREATED A NAVIGATIONAL STRATEGY THAT ATTEMPTED TO KEEP ALL SECTIONS AVAILABLE AT ALL TIMES. THIS WAS A DEPARTURE FROM THE "GOING DOWN INTO FOLDERS TO FIND THE CONTENT" MODEL, TO A MODEL WHERE EVERYTHING IS AVAILABLE FROM ANY POINT – SO ALL YOU ARE DOING IS OPENING THE CONTENT, RATHER THAN SEEKING IT.'
Tomas Roope.

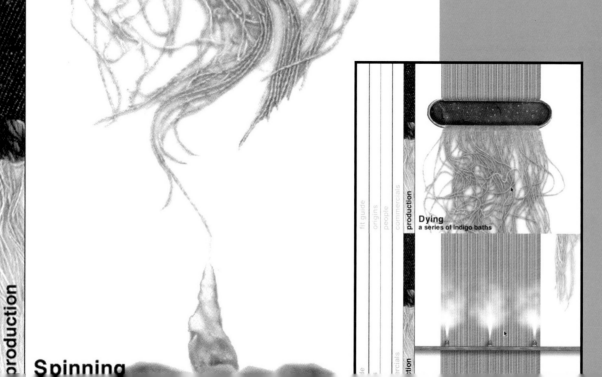

Dying
a series of indigo baths

THE BRIEF:

In April 1996 Antirom was briefed by Levi Strauss & Co. to produce an in-store interactive kiosk that would be installed across Europe in late 1996. This was the company's first major commercial project. The main objectives outlined by Levi's were:

• To create an additional communications vehicle for the brand, and thus support and extend existing communications.

• To bring a unique and exciting new element to the Original Levi's Store shopping experience, and thereby enhance the appeal of the Original Levi's Store to the core target market.

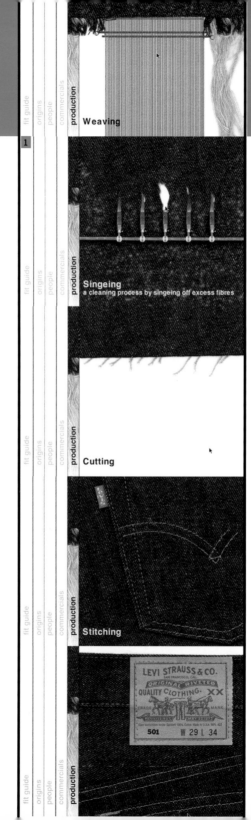

Weaving

Singeing
a cleaning process by singeing off excess fibres

Cutting

Stitching

LEVI STRAUSS & CO.
SAN FRANCISCO, CAL.
ORIGINAL RIVETED
QUALITY CLOTHING. XX
501 W 29 L 34

The first Antirom CD-ROM, funded by the Arts Council, is a series of interactive scenarios, mixing music and images. The Levi's kiosk project draws on the group's experience and ideas developed in their own personal work while working with Macromedia Director. It's inventive and witty, engaging the user through a process of discovery. As Tomas Roope says: 'It's about surprise and holding things back. Sometimes there's a fallacy that multimedia should be 100 per cent functional, but the best films make you work at them and in the end the rewards are that much greater.' In the photo-booth picture, running the cursor over the picture animates it (the girl sticks her tongue out) and the text throws up another randomly generated 'truism'.

1

In this example – 'Singeing' – rolling the cursor over the flame increases its intensity.

The other crucial aspect to consider was the issue of 'approachability' to the kiosk – if the average user only spent 70 seconds at the kiosk it was important that they felt in control of the experience and the environment as quickly as possible. Drawing on the techniques evolved in more experimental work, cursor movement was used to control aspects of sound and image rather than the straightforward 'click and wait' of most current interactive media. As a result, any movement of the mouse activates something happening on the screen or on the soundtrack. Scrollers, as well as sound mixing based upon the user's mouse movements, were extensively employed to allow the user to create their own 'journey' through the branded content. In this way they remain in intimate and constant control all the way through.

Levi's had already determined five areas of content for the kiosk that had to be covered and these categories were used as a way of dividing the content.

PRODUCTION

The quality of the products is re-emphasized by a look at the way they are produced stressing the care that goes into them. Collectively Antirom felt that this was one of the strongest sections as it combined a linear story (the manufacture of jeans from cotton) with an interactive approach which succeeds in holding the attention of the user.

Jeans for women
501®
regular
Button Fly

origins | people | production | commercials | **fit guide** | LeViS | LeViS

FITS GUIDE

This is a functional tool for people to browse the various Levi's jeans available in-store. People can see how they look, and how the different lines compare. It also works as a direct aid to making a sale.

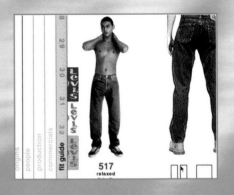

517
relaxed

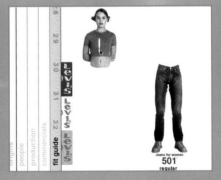

517
relaxed

DEVELOPING THE IDEA:

Research by Levi's on their previous in-store kiosks revealed that the average user would spend around 70 seconds using it before moving on. This became a fundamental issue within Antirom's design. Navigation would have to be intuitive, as well as minimal. This would require a radically simple interactive structure that meant the experience, however brief, was easy and enjoyable for the user. The key to designing the content was one of surprise and exploration, the user is drawn in to 'see what happens next'.

1940's
Levi's jeans are hard to find

1886
The two horse design brand
leather patch is introduced

HISTORY

A sense of history has always been an integral part of Levi's branding. This
section was seen as a way of reinforcing 'the original and definitive' status of
the brand. A way of locating the source of this history is in the fabric of the
jeans themselves – the product is the history.

Macromedia Director has evolved into the
most widely used multimedia authoring tool
for desktop computers. Part of its
appeal is the control it offers over graphics,
music, narration, sound effects and digital
video, as well as the interactive element that
allows the user to make selections and
choices over what happens next.
Director is controlled by a series of script,
cast and score windows, specifying the
elements to be included, what happens in
reaction to cursor movements
and so on. The key to interactivity and part
of the difficulty in using Director is Lingo,
Director's built-in programming language.
But as Tomas Roope says: 'Without Director,
something like this project just wouldn't
be possible.'

technique

*Much interactive media,
whether it's kiosk- or Web-
based, ignores the fact that
the average user only stays
long enough to see a small
fraction of the content. So it's
crucial to a project's success
that, however short a period
a user stays, they retain a
sense of satisfaction from the
interaction.*

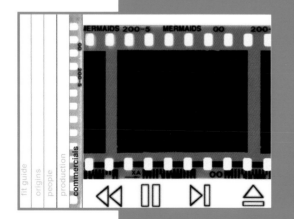

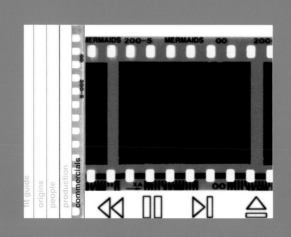

COMMERCIALS

Research had shown that the Levi's commercials were an extremely popular part of previous kiosk projects. Antirom extended this idea bringing extra value to the section. Not only was the user able to control the playback of the commercials through an interface imitating the controls of a home VCR, but there was additional information: behind-the-scenes footage about 'the making of the commercial'. The use of MPEG compressed video meant a fast, high-quality playback.

fit guide · origins · commercials · production · **people**

STREET

Through this section Levi's wanted to express its unique brand attitude, and reinforce the core values of its products – youth, independence, and so on. Antirom interviewed a wide range of people in an empty shop in London's Soho district, videoing from several angles simultaneously. The video was cut into short clips, each containing three synchronous views of the same question and answer session. They filmed on the streets in the same way. The resulting video tracks were placed in an engine which allowed the user to click on the frame and cut from one shot to another, in real time.

fit guide · origins · commercials · production · **people**

SOFTWARE/HARDWARE

DIRECTOR
PHOTOSHOP
SOUNDEDIT
DEBABELISER
POWERMACS

WORKING PROCESS

THE PROJECT DRAWS TOGETHER A RANGE OF VISUAL AND INFORMATIVE RESOURCES FROM DIFFERENT MEDIA AND COMBINES THEM INTO A SINGLE INTERACTIVE PIECE. THE ABILITY TO COMBINE THE DISPARATE ELEMENTS SUCH AS STILL IMAGES, VIDEO, SOUND AND TEXT INTO ONE EASILY-UNDERSTOOD INTERFACE GIVES THE PIECE ITS STRENGTH.

ANTIROM
29–35 LEXINGTON STREET • LONDON
W1R 3HQ • UK

CLIENTS INCLUDE: BBC; MTV; Toyota; Ford; Guinness. **[SEE PAGE 145]**

12. THE ATTIK DESIGN
NOISE [3]

COMPANY BACKGROUND:

THE ATTIK DESIGN WAS FOUNDED IN 1986 BY SIMON NEEDHAM AND JAMES SOMMERVILLE BASED IN HUDDERSFIELD. IN THE PERIOD SINCE, THEY HAVE OPENED OFFICES IN LONDON AND NEW YORK, AND HAVE A RANGE OF CLIENTS FROM MTV TO FIRST DIRECT.

'24

First Direct is really a very simple idea. Let people design their own bank – they can bank when they want to, where they want to and how they want to. Even our accounts and

first direct

first direct

first direct

First Direct is no more than a quickly changing amoeba shaped by its environment and its customers. How then is it held together? Its heart is a set of values, shared by the people working within it and communicated externally via our brand. This set of values, our culture, focuses on building values for our customers through engaging in an open dialogue with them. Its brain is our database, a highly effective piece of wiring which enables us to track that intelligent dialogue on a one-on-one basis and tells us where we are creating value. With such a simple structure, we need a simple design framework to express our form and function. We might be communicating day or night, by mail, telephone or PC, about a multitude of services. Yet we need an innate straight forwardness, with space to express our intangibility, but with strength to give us substance. This directness is expressed in our black and white base framework, with our logo 'first direct' firmly to the fore. Around this our preference is for strong colours, intelligent visuals and a modernity which points our way forward to an exhilarating future. Indicative of an open style of banking and people with open minds.

PROJECT CREDITS:

DESIGN   THE
ATTIK DESIGN

THE BRIEF:

Attik publishes a series of showcase titles, Noise, combining work for clients with designs especially created for the project. The books mix an unashamed brashness about the group's talents with wry humour. For the designers at Attik, it's an opportunity to take the way they work and the work they produce to its limits. Attik's director, Simon Needham, says of the latest in the series currently in production, Noise [3]:

'IT IS EXPECTED TO GENERATE MORE WORLDWIDE RECOGNITION AND LOTS OF FAME AND CASH.'

PROJECT [1]

ASSIMILATING PEOPLE'S REACTIONS TO THE PREVIOUS ATTIK PUBLICATION, NOISE [2]

Symbols related to a change in direction.

A collaboration of images and text which epitomize the reactions and comments of designs produced for Noise [2], the Attik's previous publication, which will be incorporated in the Attik publication, Noise [3].

The image conveys a mystical feeling combining the accumulation of burnt wood, black and white mark-making exercises and handwritten Thai text extracted from the insides of old paper bags. The main portrait is of a young, dual-nationality girl (Thai–British), alongside visual symbols and other found images. Overall, this is an eclectic design with a particular message to appreciate mark-making and experimentation.

A parody relating Noise [2] as a design manual with a Swiss army knife (something for everyone), in the setting of an old woman's attic. The basic aim is to portray the beginning of many styles and influences.

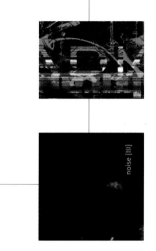

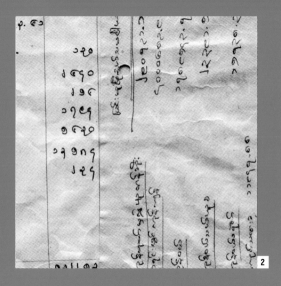

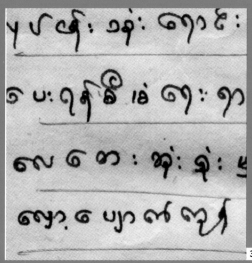

1
A self-portrait [Gabrielle Hansen].

2 – 3
Handwritten Thai text.

USE OF TECHNOLOGY:

The initial images were gathered as raw material from various locations. They were then photographed and scanned in using Agfa DuoScan and Scan maker 2.

The images were then collated using Adobe PhotoShop 3.05 on various layers to achieve the main background image. The text information and graphic symbols were created in FreeHand 5.5 and exported into Adobe PhotoShop to complete the image.

Final artwork was created in FreeHand 5.5.

PROJECT [2]

POSTCARD FROM GREECE

'As part of the compulsory national service that all males over 18 have to fulfil, "Postcard From Greece" is a collaboration of correspondence spanning two years in the life of an army soldier.'

'Mostly typographic in content, the design is an illustration of the harsh and angry reaction of the sender to his desperate situation. The background is totally derived from the distortion of actual letters sent, as a reflection of the way in which the situation has changed the soldier's control over his life. In contrast, the editorial is layed out in a strict, regimental manner.'

technique

Attik's self-published titles, Noise, give their in-house designers the freedom that isn't always possible in a project for a commercial client. The ideas that develop in this context are then allowed to inform all their later work.

1
The process of type distortion.

2
Elements that made up the final layered image.

3
Initial stages.

4
The completed project.

postcard from greece

9.95.

4

2

3

USE OF TECHNOLOGY:

Actual text from handwritten and typed letters was scanned in using Agfa DuoScan and Scan maker 2. The images were then distorted and layered together using the photocopier, hand-rolled ink and PhotoShop filters, to give the effect of distorted camouflage.

Main background image assembled in PhotoShop 3.05.

Final artwork was created in FreeHand 5.5.

PROJECT [3]

CAR CRIME

'My spread concerning car crime came about from having my own car stolen about six months ago. I saw it as my chance to get back at certain people who didn't exactly help me when it was stolen.'

'The whole issue of car crime is a very dirty one – it was very important to get this across in my design – smooth and curvy three-dimensional type was not going to work for this one! I started by designing thumbnails in my sketch-book. I knew roughly even at this early stage what media I was going to use, it was just a case of designing the spread to look very avant-garde whilst using old procedures. I thought it was very important that my type was broken up – really rough and relatively illegible. After settling for the chosen layout, I set about designing on the computer. I started off designing the title sprawling over both pages with the letters different sizes and not all the same way up. I then printed this out. It was then a case of distressing this using mainly cellotape. This was stuck over the top of certain areas of the letters and peeled away producing a really rough dirty feel. The copy on the left page was produced in FreeHand. I wanted to get across my anger and what better way than to deconstruct a classic font. I am a great believer in creating fonts for a particular job.'

'The text on the right-hand page was initially going to be done in the same style but I thought it would be a bit too much, so I opted for Helvetica. I was able to get across my anger in different ways here. Special words were picked out and made bigger, words overlap and negative leading is used extensively. Uncomfortable line breaks and widows – stuff you are taught not to do must be done as it is challenging convention, it is something you shouldn't do – just like stealing someone's car.'

'THE MAIN AIM OF THE BRIEF WAS TO GET ACROSS THE EMOTIONS I FELT WHEN IT HAPPENED – WHEN I REALIZED THAT MY CAR WAS NOT THERE. THAT FRANTIC, EMPTY, CONFUSED THEN EXTREMELY ANGRY FEELING OF SHEER HELPLESSNESS THAT PEOPLE WERE IN MY CAR AND I COULD NOT DO ANYTHING ABOUT IT.'

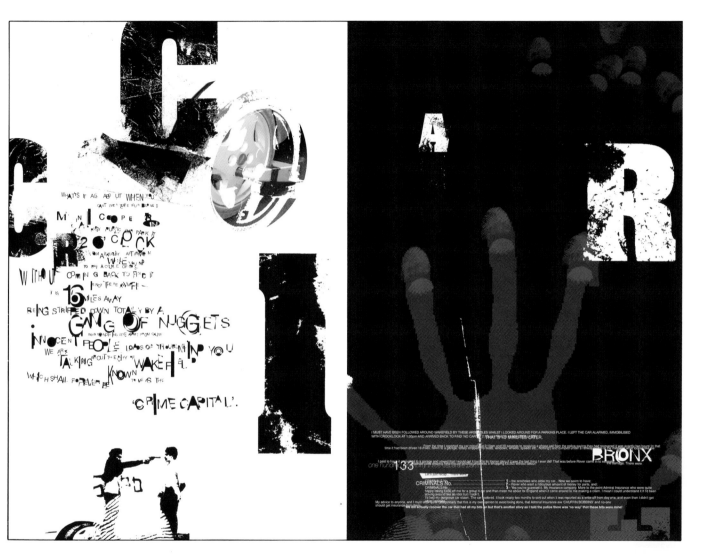

'I wanted to keep the colours simple and very bold. I used big blocks of black and large areas of white to help the design breathe. It is very easy to get too carried away and fill your spread with stuff. You have to remember that you are in charge of the reader, you tell the reader what he looks at first and how you guide him through your spread is up to you. How elements are positioned – how big they are, what colour they are – also depends on the designer.'

'The finishing touches were added using silver and spot UV varnish. By scanning in my own fingerprints I was able to print this first, beneath black, which shows through as metallic black. It gives the effect of what the police leave behind after dusting for finger-prints, as if the robbers have had their hands on my page. The spot UV is printed last everywhere where the silver isn't – by inverting the silver plate. If you have ever noticed when you touch metal or a window, where you have touched goes dull.'

1 – 10
**Details of the complex
layered file in PhotoShop.**

11
**The final computer-
generated image.**

THE COVER WAS TO BE OUR 'MOST WILD AND WACKY PIECE OF WORK'.

PROJECT [4]

The brief was to design the cover for an issue of *MacUser*. The cover was to be Attik's 'most wild and wacky piece of work'. In terms of design, the final illustration had to demonstrate what can be done using a Mac and PhotoShop, to push the boundaries and create something entirely computer-generated. The image was built up in a purely digital form using over 30 layers in PhotoShop. The amount of layers meant a huge file of almost 300Mb which was manipulated by reacting the layers with one another to create subtlety, depth and complexity within the illustration. Some of the type was manipulated in Strata StudioPro (3D software package) and then brought into PhotoShop. The finished illustration was flattened (where all the layers become one), JPEG compressed and then sent by ISDN to the client.

THE TECHNOLOGY USED:
POWER MACINTOSH 9500/120 WITH
260MB RAM, 5 GIG HARD DRIVE AND
PHOTOENGINE VIDEO CARD
21" COLOUR MONITOR
PHOTOSHOP 3.05
FREEHAND 5.5
STUDIOPRO

PROJECT [5]
TYPEFACE:
CIVILIZATION 00.00
FORMED FROM SIX ORIGINAL SYMBOLS

The Original Symbols

TIME: ADVANCE: ACHIEVE: ACCELERATE: ATTAIN: ORGANIZE: REFINE: CULTIVATE: DOMESTICATE: EDUCATE: ENLIGHTEN: DEVELOP: EVOLVE: MUTATE: ORIGINATE: COMMUNICATE: TRANSLATE: SYMBOLIZE: CIVILIZE: CONTACT.

INFLUENCE:

The Past: The Present: The Future:
Ancient Handmade Books:
Old Alphabets: Hieroglyphics: Sculptures:
Music: For an orchestra who wanted
to communicate the following:

A set of symbols that are timeless
Lost and forgotten
As ancient as the earth
Discovered and pushed into the future

First contact with an unknown civilization
An empire more advanced
More complex than any

Trying to understand, educate, translate
Too much information
Overload, interfer-
ence, noise.

SOFTWARE/HARDWARE

TYPEFACE DRAWN USING:
FREEHAND 5.01
IMAGE MANIPULATED USING:
PHOTOSHOP 3.05

LAYOUT ARRANGED IN:
FREEHAND 5.01
3D MANIPULATION:
STRATA STUDIOPRO

WORKING PROCESS

AFTER LOOKING AT A VARIETY OF OLD ALPHABETS, RUNES, SCULPTURES AND MODERN ICONS AND LOGOS, DESIGN ON THE SIX INITIAL SYMBOLS BEGAN. QUICK SKETCHES OF UNUSUAL SHAPES WERE MADE AND THESE WORKED UP IN FREEHAND 5.01 WHERE THE INITIAL ICONS BEGAN TO TAKE SHAPE. ONCE THE BASIC SHAPES WERE CREATED, THE ALPHABET WAS ROUGHLY BLOCKED OUT AND THEN TWEAKED EXTENSIVELY TO ITS PRESENT FORM. EACH LETTER-FORM IS MORE A GRAPHIC ICON IN ITSELF, MUCH LIKE THE MAJESTIC AND ORNATE ALPHABETS OF OLD.

THE ATTIK DESIGN LIMITED
41 WARPLE MEWS • WARPLE WAY
LONDON • W3 0RX • UK

CLIENTS INCLUDE: Kodak Worldwide; Channel 4;
Club 18–30; Sony Playstation; Warner Brothers and
Yorkshire Electricity. [SEE PAGE 153]

13. FAYDHERBE/DE VRINGER
[Z]OO-PRODUCTIONS 1996 DIARY

THE APPROACH:
'IN PROJECTING TRANSPARENT IMAGES ON TOP OF EACH OTHER, WE TRIED TO CREATE IMAGES THAT STILL LEAVE THINGS OPEN FOR THE READER'S IMAGINATION,' EXPLAINS WOUT DE VRINGER. 'IN OTHER WORDS, WE WANTED TO LEAVE THEM OPEN TO DIFFERENT INTERPRETATIONS. THE IMAGES FALL INTO THE SAME GRID ON EVERY SPREAD TO GIVE AN ALMOST "ACCIDENTAL" LOOK TO IT.' IN THIS WAY THE DESIGN OF THE DIFFERENT PAGES, ALTHOUGH TIGHTLY STRUCTURED, HAS A VERY FLEXIBLE FEEL TO IT.

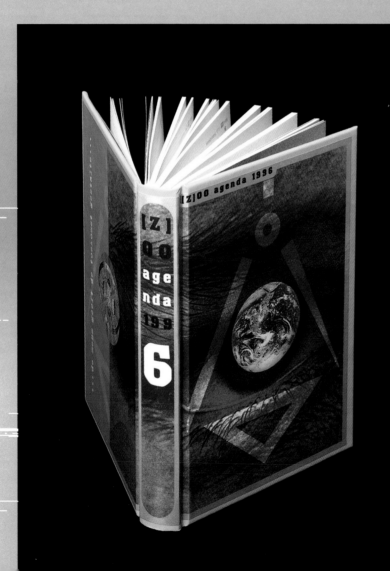

de
mens
[z]
oo
geeft
age
nda 199
de
toekomst
6
gestalte

PROJECT CREDITS:

DESIGN DIRECTORS: BEN FAYDHERBE/WOUT DE VRINGER
DESIGNERS: BEN FAYDHERBE/WOUT DE VRINGER

Ben Faydherbe and Wout de Vringer set up their studio together, having previously worked at the Vorm Vijf studio, also based in The Hague. Keeping their studio small has kept them in control and given them the flexibility to pick and choose their jobs.

THE BRIEF:

Each year, publisher [Z]OO-productions publishes a diary aimed at designers and those with an interest in design. Different designers are invited to do the job each year and because of the nature of the project, the selected designers are given almost total freedom. The only fixed things are the theme, 'Time' and the format regarding the size, binding and the use of two PMS colours for the calendar pages. The diary is sold through galleries, museums and bookshops, and because of the limited run, it has achieved a certain 'collectibility'.

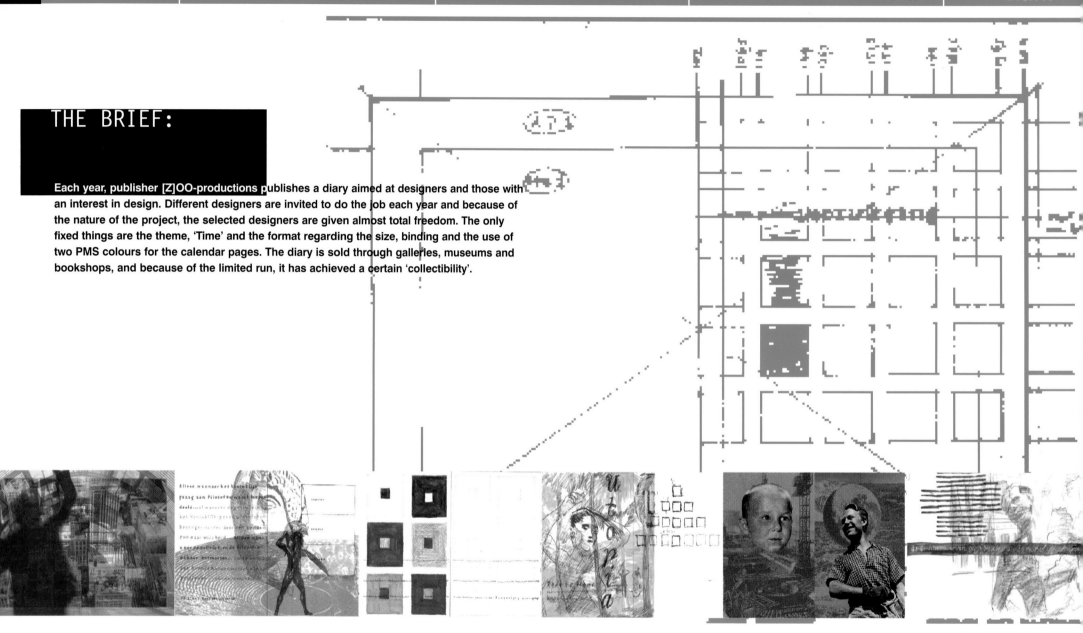

'BY USING A COLLAGE OF TEXT AND IMAGES WE WANTED TO PUT THE PROPHECIES IN A DIFFERENT CONTEXT FOR THE READER.'

onsterfelijkheid

in afwachting van   en het

aards paradijs

8e eeuw   ...taan te ontkomen

The time-line at the bottom of the spread reads '1911–1980 Philosopher Marshall McLuhan proposes that through acceleration and changes in the information process, the medium itself becomes the message.' By placing this alongside the central image of Egyptian hieroglyphics, the designers' intention is to show that not all 'new' ideas are as new as we might at first think.

THE INITIAL APPROACH:

'What we did this year,' says Faydherbe and de Vringer 'was to take prophecies from artists, philosophers and scientists from 800BC up to the 1960s as our starting point. By using a collage of text and images we wanted to put the prophecies in a different context for the reader. The images are then linked by a chronological time-line running across the bottom of each page.'

DEVELOPING THE IDEA:

'In projecting transparent images on top of each other, we tried to create images that still leave things open for the reader's imagination,' explains Ben Faydherbe. 'In other words, we wanted to leave them open to different interpretations. The images fall into the same grid on every spread to give it an almost "accidental" look.' In this way, the design of the different pages, although tightly structured, has a very flexible feel to it. Each spread is structured around the black bar at the bottom of the page with a brief explanation of the person featured and their ideas. The text in the image relates to the text in the bar but also stands on its own. Just as the images are layered to produce shifting meaning, so is the text.

The montage effect mixes images of different sizes into the transparent layers resulting in a visual richness. The use of old, sometimes antique images, is used to show that 'ideas that we think of as "modern" aren't always as original as we think; more often they're simply repetitions of old ideas and old philosophies,' says de Vringer. Similarly, contemporary images are used in combination with old ideas as a way of re-contextualizing them. To reflect the retro-futurism of the project's design, the designers used the font Trixie, a degraded typewriter face, on the images. To contrast with this, Colassalis, a modern almost self-consciously constructed face, was used in the straplines.

THE USE OF OLD, SOMETIMES ANTIQUE IMAGES, IS USED TO SHOW THAT 'IDEAS THAT WE THINK OF AS "MODERN" AREN'T ALWAYS AS ORIGINAL AS WE THINK; MORE OFTEN THEY'RE SIMPLY REPETITIONS OF OLD IDEAS AND OLD PHILOSOPHIES.'

While all the image pages in the diary conform to the same grid, the designers have made the arrangement of the elements on the page appear almost accidental. The black bar across the bottom of each page chronologically encapsulates the thoughts of philosphers and artists from Nostradamus to Marshall McLuhan. By montaging the text with layered images, designers Faydherbe and de Vringer have thrown a new light on well-known prophecies and historical moments, shifting their context and meaning.

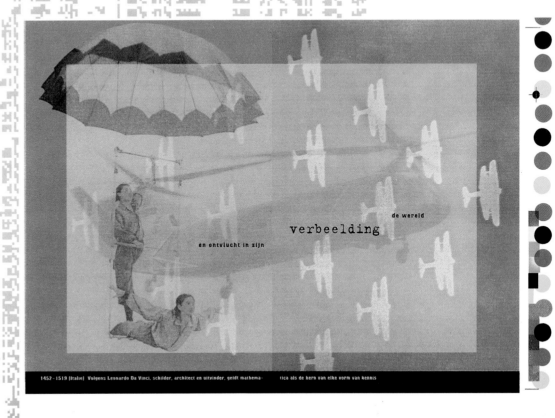

de wereld

verbeelding

en ontvlucht in zijn

1452 - 1519 (Italie) Volgens Leonardo Da Vinci, schilder, architect en uitvinder, geldt mathema-   tica als de kern van elke vorm van kennis

'BECAUSE WE WERE TAUGHT TO DESIGN WITHOUT COMPUTERS, I DON'T THINK IT HAS REALLY CHANGED OUR WAY OF THINKING.'

Geen middel, hoe vreemd het ook leek, werd onbeproefd gelaten om toch maar een glimp van de toekomst op te vangen. Priesters en profeten hebben van oudsher de beste contacten met de alziende goden van de kosmos, maar ook andere specialisten met een bijzondere begaafdheid inzake de toekomst worden geraadpleegd. Ze keken voor ons in een glazen bol, onderzochten het koffiedik of de structuur van een handvol kippebotjes. Ze lazen de lijnen van de hand en legden geheimzinnige kaarten. Nog altijd. Helderzienden adverteren hun vaardigheden in de krant en in elke kiosk ligt de Enkhuizer Almanak. Horoscopen worden nog steeds getrokken en desgewenst op floppy aangeleverd. Dat de orakeltaal daarbij vervangen is door computertaal, is slechts een technisch aspect. Aan het verlangen een antwoord in de sterren te vinden is weinig veranderd.

Er zijn natuurlijk ook rationele methoden. Het geloof in de vooruitgang en de bijna onbegrensde mogelijkheden van de techniek hebben niet alleen aanleiding gegeven tot de fantasieën van Jules Verne, H.G. Wells en andere science-fiction schrijvers, maar ook tot een wetenschappelijk onderbouwd toekomstonderzoek. Vooral de dynamische en snel veranderende industriële maatschappijen van het westen hebben een grote behoefte aan scenario's van een mogelijke toekomst. Bestuurders en politici in Nederland baseren hun beleid bij voorbeeld op onderzoek van de Wetenschappelijke Raad voor het Regeringsbeleid

en de modellen en statistieken van het Centraal Planbureau. Ondernemers en handelaren richten zich op internationaal georiënteerde marktverkenners en trendvoorspellers. En de wetenschappers begeven zich ondertussen op gebieden die voorhanden alleen nog als paradoxen binnen de bestaande kennis kunnen worden ingepast.

Bij al die ideeën over hoe het zou kunnen zijn, vangen zich als vanzelf ideeën over hoe het zou behoren te worden. Niet alleen bij utopisten en wereldverbeteraars. De scheidslijn tussen de toekomst willen kennen en deze willen beheersen is vaag. Het bedrijfsleven zoekt liever trendsetters dan trendvolgers. In de politiek wordt een prognose al gauw omgezet in planning. Dat is –onder meer– een gevolg van het feit dat naast optimistische visies over een betere toekomst met meer welvaart, meer kennis en meer efficiënte maatschappelijke verhoudingen, er zich ook duidelijke nadelen aftekenden op de weg vooruit. Vooraanstaande wetenschappers, politici en kunstenaars hebben niet nagelaten op een minder rooskleurige toekomst te wijzen. Zij voorzagen verpaupering en ellende onder de arbeiders, technocratische dictaturen, een verlies aan humaniteit en uitputting van de natuurlijke bronnen. Op deze veel terechte bedenkingen en angsten reageren overheden, bedrijven en maatschappelijke organisaties met het doelbewust bijsturen van ontwikkelingen. Het idee van de maakbare samenleving is de contramal van het doemdenken. De balans tussen beide

De [Z]00-agenda wordt elk jaar door een andere ontwerper vormgegeven, ontwerpers die zich laten inspireren door het thema tijd.

Bij de [Z]00-agenda 1996 zijn twee ontwerpers betrokken, Ben Faydherbe en Wout de Vringer uit Den Haag. Zij creëeren een nieuwe context door geschriften en gedachten van denkers uit het verleden te illustreren met beeldmateriaal dat in tijdsbeeld tegengesteld is. Want door kennis van het verleden heeft de mens een idee van het heden en probeert zich een beeld te vormen van de toekomst. De kunsthistoricus en auteur Gerrit Willems toont in de begeleidende tekst aan dat dit beeld van de toekomst vaak gebaseerd is op een nostalgisch verlangen naar het verleden.

Kortom, tijd is voor een agenda niet alleen een logisch thema, het blijft mensen inspireren en bezighouden.

Dat drukwerk niet alleen in het verleden en vandaag maar zeker ook morgen een cruciale rol heeft gespeeld en zal blijven spelen in ons leven toont deze agenda nogmaals aan. Drukwerk is bij de verspreiding van kennis van centraal belang, het heeft de ontwikkeling van cultuur, zoals wij die vandaag beleven, mogelijk gemaakt.

De [Z]00-agenda 1996 kwam ook dit jaar weer tot stand dankzij de goede samenwerking tussen [Z]00-produkties, Club 12 Grafische Bedrijven, Grafische Cultuurstichting KVGO, Gerrit Willems en natuurlijk de ontwerpers Ben Faydherbe en Wout de Vringer.

Goed en mooi drukwerk is en blijft onmisbaar.

Frans Sprugt,
Voorzitter Grafische Cultuurstichting Koninklijk Verbond van Grafische Ondernemingen

de mens [z]oo geeft agenda 1996 de toekomst 6 gestalte

DESIGN AND TECHNOLOGY:

Although Faydherbe and de Vringer have integrated computers into their design process, much of the work is done in more traditional ways – paste-ups, scrap art and marker pens. The ideas that make up the work are developed to a very high degree before anything is done on the computer. The adoption of the Macintosh in their studio has undoubtably made their lives easier, but there hasn't been a great shift in the style of their work. As Wout de Vringer explains, 'because we were taught to design without computers, I don't think it has really changed our way of thinking, but it has made it a lot faster and easier with the computer. The main thing is that you do get to see lots of alternatives before you decide on the final one.'

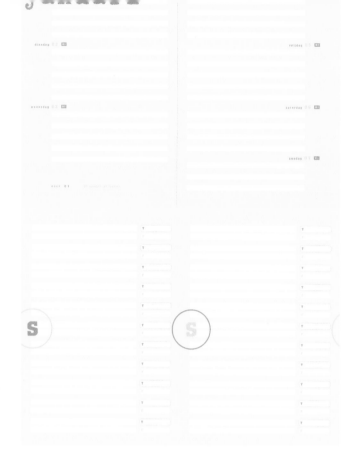

tech**nique**

Faydherbe and de Vringer work extensively with paper sketches and layouts before moving to the computer. This ability to visualize the process is integral to their approach regardless of the tools they use to realize the completed work.

SOFTWARE/HARDWARE

QUARKXPRESS
PHOTOSHOP
POWERMACS

WORKING PROCESS

FAYDHERBE AND DE VRINGER ADOPTED COMPUTERS RELATIVELY LATE ON BUT HAVE INTEGRATED THEM INTO THEIR WORKING PRACTICE ALONGSIDE THE TECHNIQUES LEARNT IN THEIR PRE-COMPUTER DAYS. A TYPICAL PROJECT WILL GO THROUGH MANY STAGES: SOME ONSCREEN, SOME ON PAPER. WHAT ALWAYS REMAINS IMPORTANT TO THEM ARE IDEAS AND THEIR REALIZATION THROUGH THE CREATIVE PROCESS.

FAYDHERBE/DE VRINGER
POSTBUS 63502 • 2502 JM DEN HAAG
THE HAGUE • THE NETHERLANDS

CLIENTS INCLUDE: FKU; Centrum Beeldende
Kunst Dordrecht; Cinematheek Haags Filmhuis.
[SEE PAGE 148]

3.1: CARLOS SEGURA/[T-26]
A NEW DIGITAL TYPE FOUNDRY:
430 QUICKTIME MOVIES

'I DON'T WANT A BIG COMPANY BECAUSE I DON'T WANT TO HAVE TO TAKE ON JOBS JUST TO PAY THE BILLS.' CARLOS SEGURA.

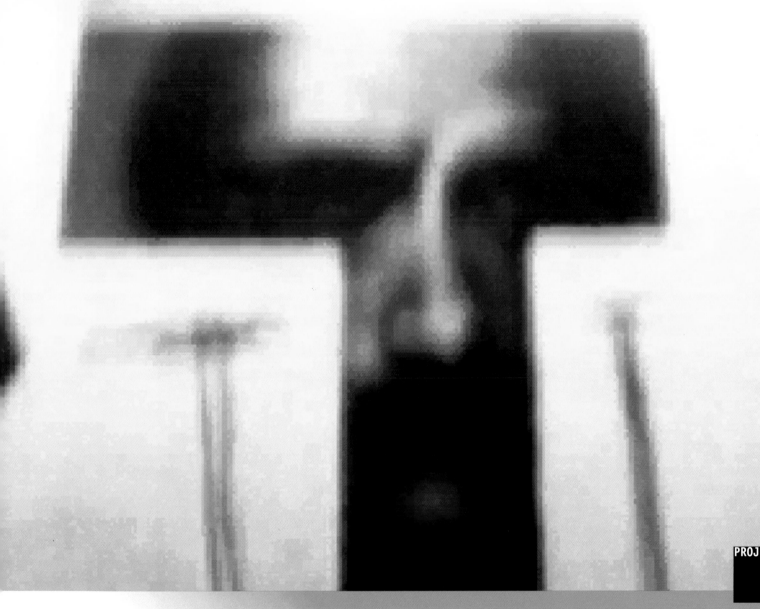

CARLOS SEGURA
CARLOS SEGURA
DAVID HEWITT
CARLOS SEGURA

THE DIVERSITY COMES FROM COMING UP ON THE AD AGENCY SIDE RATHER THAN THE DESIGN
SIDE, BUT IT DID TEACH ME HOW TO THINK DIFFERENTLY WHEN STARTING A PROJECT. I DON'T WANT
A BIG COMPANY BECAUSE I DON'T WANT TO HAVE TO TAKE ON JOBS JUST TO PAY THE BILLS.'
CARLOS SEGURA.

OMAHA : :
GODLIKE:
TIME IN HELL:
26 FACES:

The individual frames from the Omaha and Godlike QuickTime movies. The movies are supplied free to customers when they purchase a font library on CD.

Born out of the frustrations of a 13-year career in advertising, Carlos Segura set up Segura Inc. in 1991 to 'pursue design and its tangible and personal possibilities'. Its clients range from the funky XXX Snowboards to Harley-Davidson. Carlos Segura's constant pursuit of the experimental led to the foundation of a new digital type foundry [T-26] in 1994. As Carlos Segura says: 'Communication that doesn't take a chance, doesn't stand a chance.'

'SO I WAS LOOKING FOR SOMETHING TO DO AS WELL AND IF PEOPLE LIKED IT, THAT WAS FINE AND IF THEY DIDN'T, THAT WAS FINE TOO.'

'In 1991 I quit the ad agency business where I'd been an art director and set up Segura Inc. which was a wonderful release because I had always wanted to inject as much fine art as possible into the commercial work. When I set up [T-26] in 1994 it was a by-product of frustration with clients constantly looking over your shoulder telling you to make the logo bigger. So I was looking for something to do as well and if people liked it, that was fine and if they didn't, that was fine too. I believe that [T-26] has grown because of the way we present our product line – the point of view that nothing we do negates anything else and that there's enough room in this world for all of us to do whatever we do. We also didn't want to start a foundry and do the same stuff that everyone else was doing. The category we created was being ignored by the major foundries.'

THE LATEST [T-26] PROJECT STARTED IN 1995 – DESCRIBED BY CARLOS SEGURA AS 'A DIGITAL DIRECT MAIL CAMPAIGN' – AND CONSISTS OF 430 QUICKTIME MOVIES, ONE ON EACH OF THE **[T-26]** FONTS. IN EFFECT, IT'S A SERIES OF MUSIC PROMOTIONAL VIDEOS FOR THE FOUNDRY'S TYPEFACES.

R *2 Time in Hell

'Part of the catalyst for the project was Hat Nguyen doing some QuickTime movies for some of his fonts, and that triggered the thought that maybe we should do it as a serious thing, as a way of promoting typography. It's quite difficult to build a music video for something that doesn't exist. We either have to base it on the name of the font or the style of the font. The only problem at the moment is the size of the files, so although they're only 15 frames a second (320 x 240 resolution), the files can be 80Mbs.'

'We start with the music track, which may be one of our own pieces or someone else's we have taken, sampled and edited. We build and collect images that are appropriate for each of the movie's sections and then build it from that. Most of the pieces are already in digital form, whether it's artwork or film, and we've just started working with the Sony Digital Video cameras with digital capture boards.'

TIME IN HELL

$29.00

A NEW FONT FROM T-26

1.888.T-26.FONT

T0116

The individual frames from the [T-26] promotional QuickTime movie.

'WE'VE FOUND IT EASIER TO MAKE THE MOVIE BEFORE ASKING AN ARTIST FOR COPYRIGHT BECAUSE UNTIL THEY'VE SEEN WHAT A QUICKTIME FONT MOVIE LOOKS LIKE THEY DON'T REALLY KNOW WHAT WE'RE TALKING ABOUT. HOPEFULLY THEY GIVE PERMISSION, IF NOT WE USE SOMETHING ELSE. WE ALSO WANT TO PROMOTE NEW ARTISTS, PHOTOGRAPHERS AND MUSICIANS. IT'S LIKE A FAMILY AFFAIR.'

The elements for the movie are put together using Adobe Premiere.

'When customers purchase the type library on CD we burn a CD for them and try to include as many of the QuickTime movies on it as possible.'

'We're having a great time doing this because it's quite hard coming up with a music video for a font. Anyone who wants to do a movie for us on any of our fonts can do so. We've got an international call for entries on our Web site.'

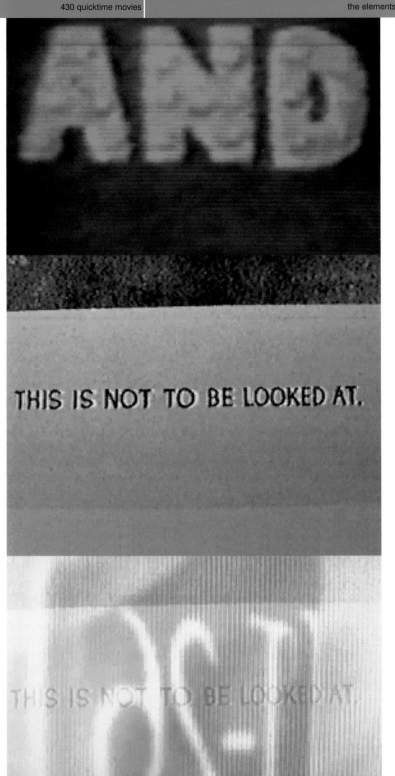

Individual frames from the [T-26] promotional QuickTime movie.

WORDS IN YOUR FACE

IN

give

2

WORDS IN YOUR FACE

'As a firm, we are seriously computer-orientated but no more than any other firm in the industry, we just happen to have a reputation as "digital guys". The truth of the matter is that we try to use the computer as a tool, as just an avenue to make something happen. I have a problem with designers who work for me who simply use it as a crutch to create something and they can't see anything but the screen. We just happen to use the computer well enough to make it feel like the computer is our only control but in fact it isn't.'

'The way I work and design isn't the traditional way with sketches first. I do it all in my head and either apply it organically by hand – painting something or folding something – or take it to the computer. I am a firm believer in the computer. The problem is that the average client believes that anyone with a computer can now be a designer.'

DESIGN AND TECHNOLOGY:

AIDING PROJECT:
'Aiding' is an ongoing project with all proceeds from sales of specially designed icons that are issued quarterly as a set of dingbats (Aid=Aids Ding=dingbats) going to Aids charities in the States. There is an international call for entries on the [T-26] Web site and in the catalogues. Contributions have already come in from some of the finest designers in the world.

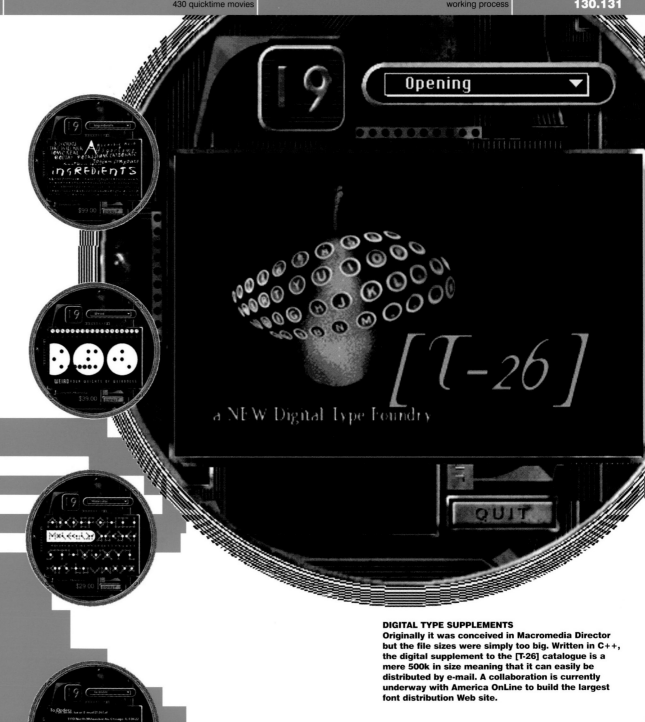

DIGITAL TYPE SUPPLEMENTS
Originally it was conceived in Macromedia Director but the file sizes were simply too big. Written in C++, the digital supplement to the [T-26] catalogue is a mere 500k in size meaning that it can easily be distributed by e-mail. A collaboration is currently underway with America OnLine to build the largest font distribution Web site.

IJKLMNO
QRSTUVWXYZ)
efghijklmnopqrstuvwxyz]
123456789}

IJKLMNOPQRSTUVWXYZ(abcdefghijklmnopqrstuvwxyz)

The QuickTime movies that accompany the fonts of the [T-26] type foundry add a unique element that no one else is currently offering. As well as being an original advertising and promotion tool, they illustrate various uses of the fonts and allow the designer a real freedom to 'do whatever they want'.

TIME IN HELL:
This font by Carlos Segura is a combination of the attributes of two classic typefaces – Times and Helvetica. The original artwork is drawn in Adobe Illustrator and then imported into Fontographer to finish it off where the kerning and metrics are worked out before the final font is generated. The postcard is part of the promotional material that is shipped with the catalogue showing the font in use. The figure of the man is made up of the letters from the font.

SOFTWARE/HARDWARE

PHOTOSHOP
FONTOGRAPHER
ILLUSTRATOR
FREEHAND
PREMIERE

WORKING PROCESS

THE RISE OF THE COMPUTER HAS LED TO THE CREATION
OF MOVIES ON THE DESKTOP IN THE SAME WAY THAT IT
MADE DESKTOP PUBLISHING POSSIBLE. WITH A RELA-
TIVELY INEXPENSIVE SET-UP, A SMALL DESIGN STUDIO CAN
PRODUCE WORK IN A RANGE OF DIFFERENT MEDIA.

SEGURA INC.
1110 NORTH MILWAUKEE AVENUE
CHICAGO • ILLINOIS 60622.4017 • USA

CLIENTS INCLUDE: Q101 Radio; MRSA Architects;
TVT Records; WaxTrax Records; MTV Networks; Geffen
Records; XXX Snowboards; Virgin Interactive; The
Alternative Pick. **[SEE PAGE 152]**

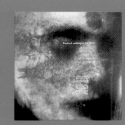

3.1: TOMATO
A PROJECT FOR *GRAPHICS*, THE ELECTRONIC WORKSHOP

COMPANY BACKGROUND:

Tomato formed in early 1991, a collection of friends with experience in graphic design, video and music, setting up together and seeing what happened next. Their current client list covers the globe: they've produced commercials for Levi's, Nike, Adidas and Pepsi; the title sequence for the film *Trainspotting*; TV titles and identities; radio commercials and print work from logos to album covers.

THE BRIEF:

In response to the RotoVision brief, John Warwicker at Tomato supplied this text and accompanying project based around a sequence of images produced for a promo for a new TV series of 'The Hunger'.

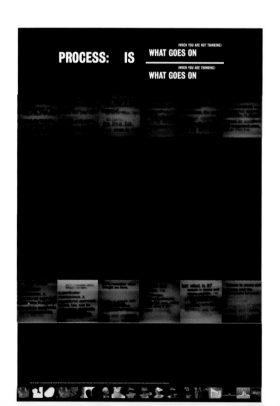

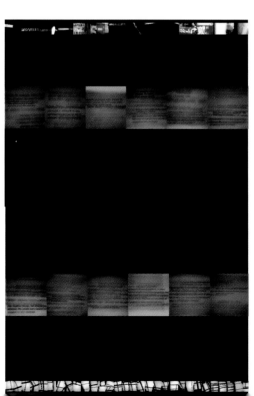

'THERE IS NO SUCH THING AS THE TOTAL PICTURE. EVERY PIECE OF MATTER EFFECTS AND INFORMS ALL OTHER PIECES OF MATTER.'

almost 30 years ago the creative team of charles and ray eames produced a film called 'powers of ten'. the film begins with a close-up shot of a man sleeping on a golf course in florida (a scene one metre wide, viewed from above, one metre away). the camera pulls back at a rate of 1010 metres per second. the man becomes a speck. the golf course soon disappears. you are now above continental america, the whole earth is within our view. soon that is gone, our galaxy is within other galaxies, then it is back once more (at the same rate) through the man's skin and eventually to the atoms themselves. this film elegantly demonstrates the interrelation of everything, and showed that what you saw depended on your position within the universe. no single viewpoint gives you the total picture. there is no such thing as the total picture. every piece of matter effects and informs all other pieces of matter. the same model applies to contemporary culture. an idea holds its attraction until it encounters the greater gravitational pull of a more persuasive one. as in quantum physics, weak attractions also have a vital role to play in shaping the universe; forces and perceptions are not only quantifiable physical manifestations that exist in relation to each other but are also interpreted through emotional and individual experience. as in the physical universe, contemporary culture is expanding at an ever increasing rate, but as it does so it deconstructs itself proportionately. it's as if the speed of the eames film is in itself increasing by the power of 10, to the point of collapse because you are now travelling so fast it is impossible to tell what speed you are travelling at. the hierarchy of scale becomes flattened and a new physics evolves. the complexity reveals more complexity. there are no neutral witnesses; culture, product, media and the individual are all bound together through mutual awareness and definition. there is no single set of physical rules about culture, there are many. the formal simplicity of this film underlines the complexity of its message.

PROJECT CREDITS:

TOMATO

TOMATO
29–35 LEXINGTON STREET • LONDON
W1R 3HQ • UK

CLIENTS INCLUDE: Levi's; Adidas; Nike; Pepsi; BBC.
[SEE PAGE 154]

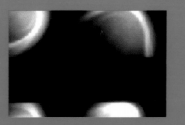

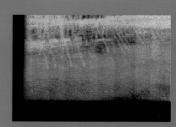

PROCESS: **IS** $\dfrac{\text{(WHEN YOU ARE NOT THINKING)}}{\text{(WHEN YOU ARE THINKING)}}$ **WHAT GOES ON**

WHAT GOES ON

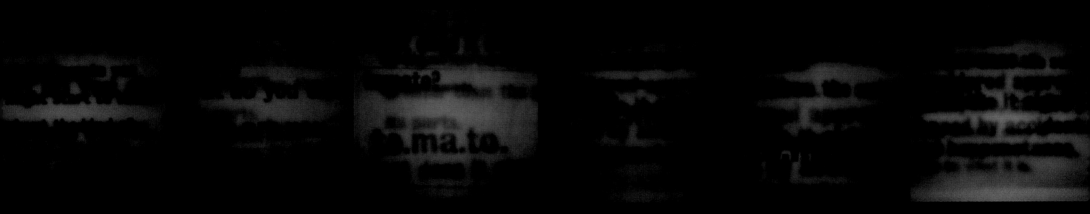

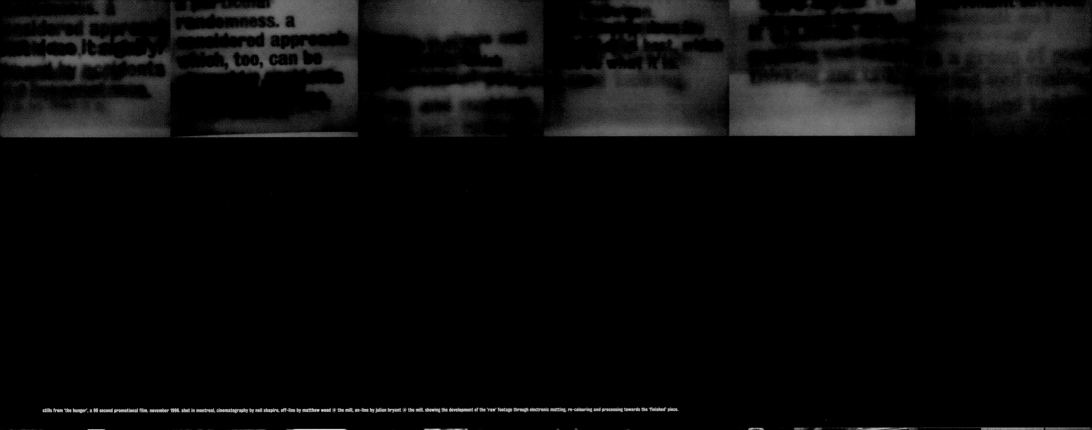

randomness. a

considered approach which, too, can be

stills from 'the hunger', a 90 second promotional film. november 1996. shot in montreal, cinematography by neil shapiro, off-line by matthew wood @ the mill, on-line by julian bryant @ the mill. showing the development of the 'raw' footage through electronic matting, re-colouring and processing towards the 'finished' piece.

'the hunger'

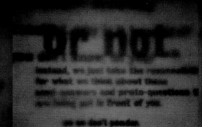

I'm trying think. I'm
trying to talk. to
communicate. am I
getting through?

It is a group of people
working and making.
thinking and talking.

or not.

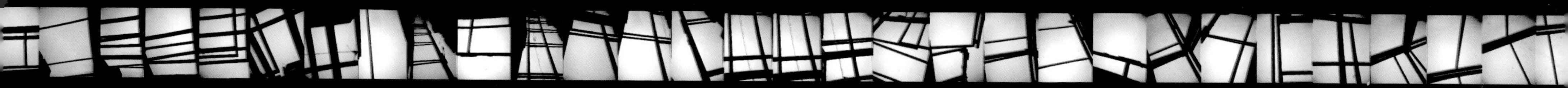

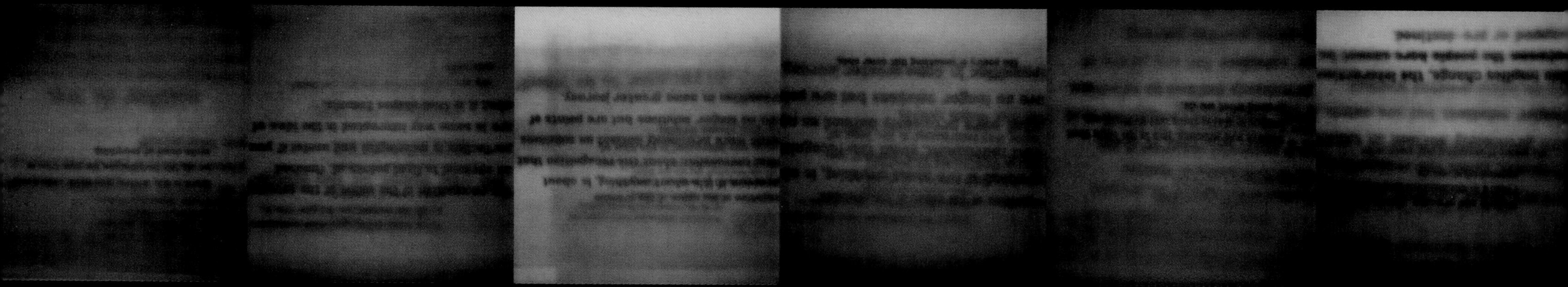

ABOUD SODANO

STUDIO 7, 10/11 ARCHER STREET,
LONDON W1V 7HG, UK.
CLIENTS INCLUDE: *Art direction/design*: Terrence Higgins
Trust; Design Museum, London; Issey Miyake, Japan; Sony
Music. *Photography*: British Telecom; Conde Nast; Macys,
New York; Calvin Klein.

1 **POSTER FOR NAN GOLDIN RETROSPECTIVE**
Whitney Museum of American Art.

2 **CONSUMER PRODUCTS PAGE DIVIDER**
For I.D. magazine's Annual Awards Issue.

3 **TERRENCE HIGGINS TRUST POSTCARDS**

4 **R. NEWBOLD BROCHURE COVER**

AMXDIGITAL

VICTORIA HOUSE, 64 PAUL STREET,
LONDON EC2A 4NA, UK.
CLIENTS INCLUDE: CompuServe; Warner Music; Saatchi &
Saatchi; Ogilvy & Mather; Lowe Howard-Spink; Paramount
Pictures.

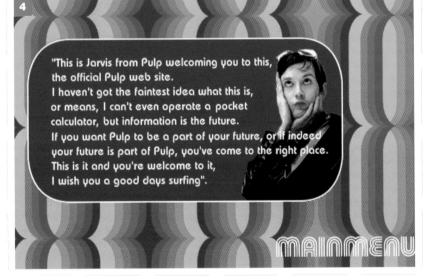

"This is Jarvis from Pulp welcoming you to this, the official Pulp web site.
I haven't got the faintest idea what this is, or means, I can't even operate a pocket calculator, but information is the future.
If you want Pulp to be a part of your future, or if indeed your future is part of Pulp, you've come to the right place. This is it and you're welcome to it, I wish you a good days surfing".

1 IMAGE BANK BROWSER (CD-ROM)
FOR KODAK

2 WEB SITE FOR MALIBU RUM
FOR LOWE HOWARD-SPINK

3 WEB SITE FOR GUINNESS BREWING
FOR OGILVY & MATHER

4 WEB SITE FOR THE BAND PULP

ANTIROM

29–35 LEXINGTON STREET,
LONDON W1R 3HQ, UK
CLIENTS INCLUDE: BBC; MTV; Toyota; Ford; Guinness.

My elbow
has the tensile strength of steel.

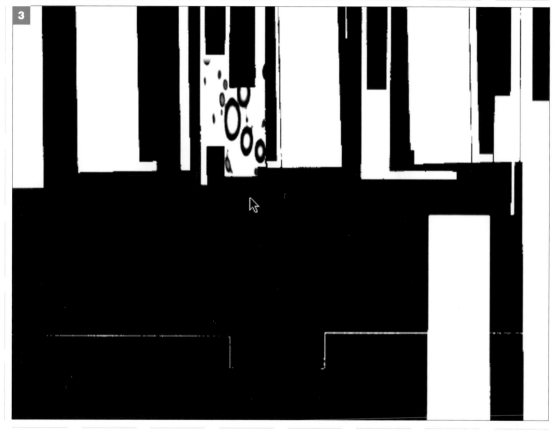

1 THE FIRST ANTIROM CD-ROM FUNDED
BY THE ARTS COUNCIL

2 ANTIROM CD-ROM FOR THE JAM
EXHIBITION AT THE BARBICAN, LONDON

3 CD-ROM FOR CREATIVE REVIEW
MAGAZINE

4 THE FIRST ANTIROM CD-ROM

AUTOMATIC

15 IRVING STREET, LEICESTER SQUARE,
LONDON WC2H 7AU, UK.

CLIENTS INCLUDE: MTV Europe; Ogilvy & Mather; Roose &
Partners; Warner Music; nu-media research; Routledge;
Cartlidge Levene; Syzygy; Tinderbox; Bob Baxter/Amalgam
and Equator International.

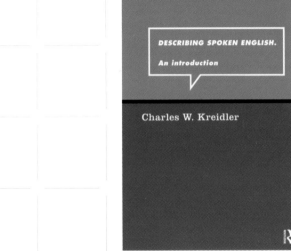

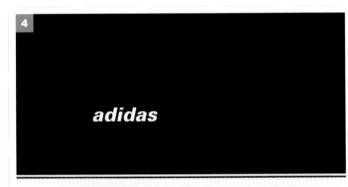

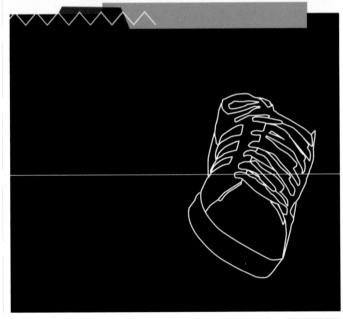

1 **ENTRE NOUS MENU**
Folded menu as part of a new identity and range
of subsidiary items for the sandwich bar 'entre nous'.

2 **ROUTLEDGE BOOK COVER**
Book cover commissioned by Routledge for
Describing Spoken English by Charles W. Kreidler.

3 **SAPPHIRE CD**
Promo-only CD covers commissioned by
Warner Music for 'never be lonely again' by
sapphire.

4 **EXPERIMENTAL WORK**
Images for an exploration of trainer love.

DOLPHIN

32 NEAL STREET, COVENT GARDEN,
LONDON, WC2H 9PS, UK.
CLIENTS INCLUDE: Epic Records; Levi Strauss (UK) Ltd.;
Harvey Nichols; Deconstruction Records.

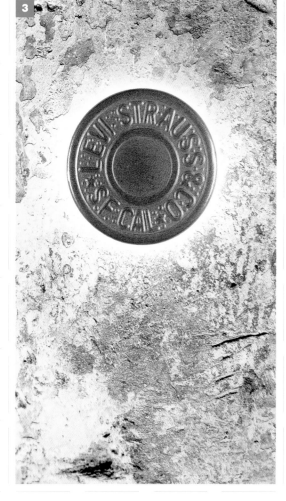

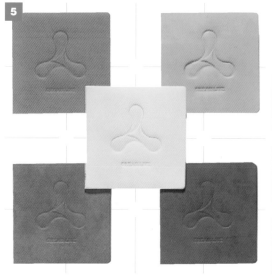

1 **LIBERATION 'CD2' IMAGE**
Part of a campaign for Pet Shop Boys singles.

2 **HARVEY NICHOLS CHRISTMAS BROCHURE**
Front cover image from the Harvey Nichols 1994 Christmas gift brochure.

3 **LEVI'S IN-STORE GRAPHICS**
One of a series of lightbox images produced for Levi's flagship store in London.

4 **LIGHTNING SEEDS ALBUM COVER**
Front cover image from the Lightning Seeds album, 'Jollification', part of a campaign.

5 **CREAM CD PACKAGING**
Part of a corporate identity, advertising and promotional campaign for a major nightclub – the CD covers are made of rubber with the logo embossed.

FAYDHERBE/
DE VRINGER

POSTBUS 63502, 2502 JM DEN HAAG, THE
HAGUE, THE NETHERLANDS.
CLIENTS INCLUDE: FKU; Centrum Beeldende Kunst
Dordrecht; Cinematheek Haags Filmhuis.

1 DE OPSTAND DER DINGEN POSTER
Poster for De opstand der dingen (Group art show). Client: Centrum Beeldende Kunst Dordrecht, size: A2 printing: Full-colour offset printing.

2 DANIEL LIBESKIND BROCHURE
Front cover for a catalogue about a project by architect Daniel Libeskind. Client: Centrum Beeldende Kunst Dordrecht, size: 164mm x 280mm printing: 2 PMS-colours and black.

3 DE DRUIVEN VAN ZEUXIS CATALOGUE
Front cover for a group show catalogue, De Druiven van Zeuxis (The grapes of Zexis). Client: FKU size: A5 printing: Black and gold.

4 TRANSPARANTE HERINNERINGEN
Front cover of a catalogue
Client: Karola Pezzarro, size: 210mm x 115mm, printing: full colour off-set printing

GREIMANSKI LABS

APRIL GREIMAN, 620 MOULTON AVENUE,
SUITE 211, LOS ANGELES, CA 90031, USA.
CLIENTS INCLUDE: California Institute of Architecture;
US West; Coop Himmelblau; Icon Shoes Corporation.

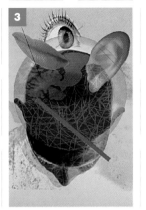

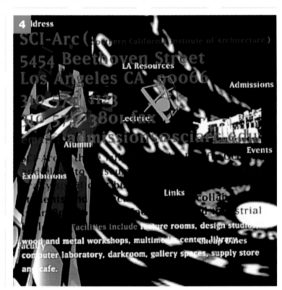

JOHNSON BANKS

STUDIO 6, 92 LOTS ROAD, LONDON
SW10 0QD, UK.
CLIENTS INCLUDE: British Telecom; The Victoria and Albert
Museum; Polygram Records; the Red Cross.

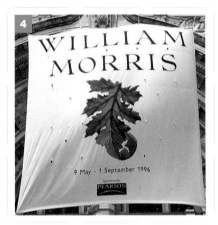

1   **MONOTYPE TYPOGRAPHY**
Corporate logotype design.

2   **SOUTH EASTERN TRAINS**
One of a series of public information posters.

3   **CHIMPS IN WIGS**
Poster for an exhibition of work by David
O'Higgins.

4   **WILLIAM MORRIS BANNER**
Part of an overall corporate scheme for an
exhibition at The Victoria and Albert Museum.

5   **DESIGN AND ART DIRECTION**
ANNUAL COVER
The jacket is made from formed plastic and has a real
stitched-in zip.

PENTAGRAM DESIGN

204 FIFTH AVENUE, NEW YORK,
NY 10010, USA.
CLIENTS INCLUDE: American Institute of Architects;
Bausch & Lomb; Cirque du Soleil; Fuji; JP Morgan;
Liz Claiborne; Phillips Van Heusen; Samsung; Texaco;
United Airlines.

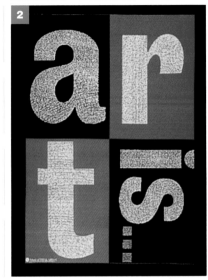

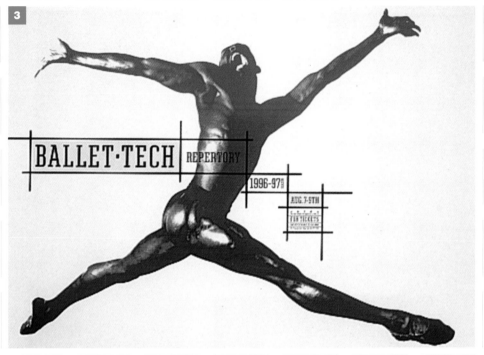

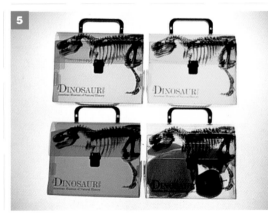

1/5 AMERICAN MUSEUM OF NATURAL HISTORY DINOSAUR MERCHANDISE PROMOTIONS 1995
Partner/designer: Paula Scher. Designers: Lisa Mazur, Jane Mella. The re-opening of the Dinosaur Halls inspired a new banner for the museum's façade and a line of retail merchandise which have contributed to a surge in profits for the institution.

2 SCHOOL OF VISUAL ARTS 'ART IS…' POSTER
Partner/designer/calligrapher: Paula Scher. One in a series of posters with the theme 'Art Is', created by various designers, illustrators, and artists to commemorate the 50th anniversary of the School of Visual Arts. The poster's letters are formed from the handwritten names of all manner of artists, from Paul Gauguin to Cher.

3 BALLET-TECH IDENTITY 1996–7
Partner/designer: Paula Scher. Designers: Lisa Mazur, Anke Stohlmann. Centred on powerful images of dancers reproduced in gradated brilliant colour and typographic 'scaffolding', the new identity expresses the elegance and precision of traditional ballet infused with the contemporary artistry that characterizes Eliot Feld's choreography.

4 BASS IDENTITY AND PACKAGING
Partner/designer: Paula Scher. Designer: Lisa Mazur. The purpose of the Bass packaging programme is to introduce a new image for G.H. Bass based on the history of the company. The identity icon refers to Bass's most famous product, the Weejun moccasin, the construction of which was derived from the Native American canoe.

SEGURA INC.

1110 NORTH MILWAUKEE AVENUE,
CHICAGO, ILLINOIS 606224017, USA.
CLIENTS INCLUDE: Q101 Radio; MRSA Architects; XXX
Snowboards; The Alternative Pick; MTV Networks; Geffen
Records; Virgin Interactive; TVT Records; WaxTrax Records.

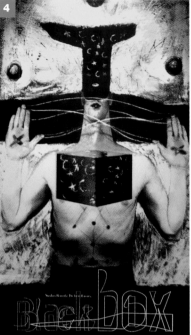

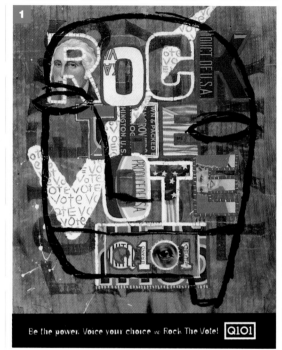

1 ROCK THE VOTE STICKER
For Q101 Radio Station.

2 FULL-PAGE NEWSPAPER ADVERT
For Q101 Radio Station.

3 CATALOGUE COVER
For XXX Snowboards, 96–97 season.

4 BLACK BOX POSTER
For record label WaxTrax Records.

THE ATTIK DESIGN

THE ATTIK DESIGN LTD., 41 WARPLE MEWS,
WARPLE WAY, LONDON W3 0RX, UK.
CLIENTS INCLUDE: Kodak Worldwide; Channel 4; Club
18–30; Sony Playstation; Warner Brothers and Yorkshire
Electricity.

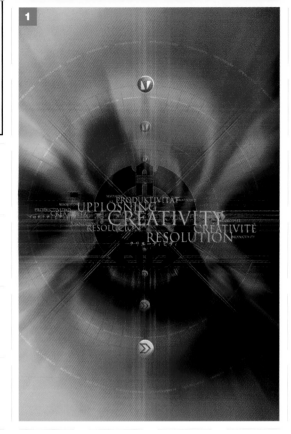

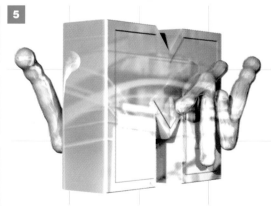

1 KODAK CINEON BROCHURE   **2** FIRST DIRECT PC BANKING CD-ROM   **3** SEGA SONIC 3D LOGO   **4** MTV NEWS PRESENTS TITLE SEQUENCE   **5** MTV REVOLVING LOGO

TOMATO

29–35 LEXINGTON STREET
LONDON W1R 3HQ, UK.
CLIENTS INCLUDE: Levi's; Nike; Adidas; Pepsi; BBC.

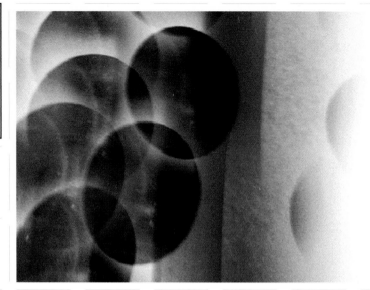

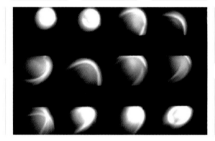

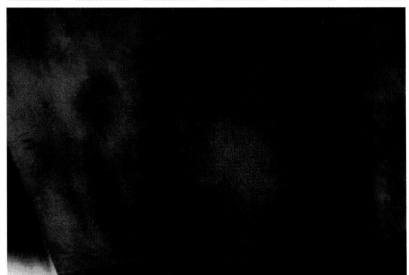

PERSONAL PROJECTS BY MEMBERS OF TOMATO 1997

VSA PARTNERS INC.

542 SOUTH DEARBORN, SUITE 202,
CHICAGO, ILLINOIS 60605, USA.
CLIENTS INCLUDE: Aetna, Inc.; Capitol Records; The Coca-
Cola Company; Einstein Bros. Bagel Company; Eastman
Kodak Company; General Motors Corporation; Nortel-
Northern Telecom; Warner Bros; Time Warner, Inc.; Potlatch
Corporation.

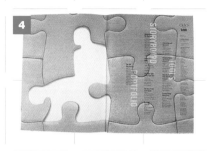

365 BEN DAYS

Potlatch

1/2 COVER AND 'TELECOMMUNICATIONS' SPREAD – A.T. KEARNEY'S 70TH ANNIVERSARY BOOK, *DEFINING MOMENTS*
Book celebrating 70 years of changing business in the 20th century. The cover is transparent vellum, the classic typography showing through from beneath. Chapter openings combine vintage and contemporary images creating a timeless feeling. The book is very subtle and the colour palette, elegant.

3/4 COVER, INSIDE FRONT GATEFOLD COVER AND PAGE ONE OF '365 BEN DAYS: A DAYPLANNER'
Promotional piece for Potlatch Corporation and its line of premium papers. VSA Partners also produced a tie-in film featuring the fictional character, Ben Day, the world's greatest designer. Besides being a dayplanner, the book is a collection of unusual facts, tips, charts, stories and anecdotes for the reader. The gatefold cover opens with a gallery of images of Ben Day in a range of poses and antics. The photographs recall images of physical comedy from the film, further personifying Ben Day as a real person. The dayplanner continues to give the reader a glimpse into the background of Ben Day – his life and his accomplishments.

5/6 COVER OF CLIO PRESENTS *THE WORK*, INSIDE FRONT COVER AND CONTENTS
A quarterly publication featuring the winners and the best advertising from around the world who competed in the Clio Awards competition. The cover photograph features one of the campaigns and the new masthead design for the magazine. A strong graphic approach and focus on award-winning work was the aim in order to heighten awareness of the publication.
A quick, easy table of contents featuring summaries of all the contributing articles helps the reader navigate and find information.
Each spread is simple and more singular with its imagery, including the pages that have advertising, to help create a more unified feeling for the publication between its contents and the advertisers who purchased space.

WEBMEDIA

2 KENDALL PLACE, LONDON W1H 3AH, UK.
CLIENTS INCLUDE: Which?; Time Out; Reader's Digest;
BBC; Sony Music Europe.

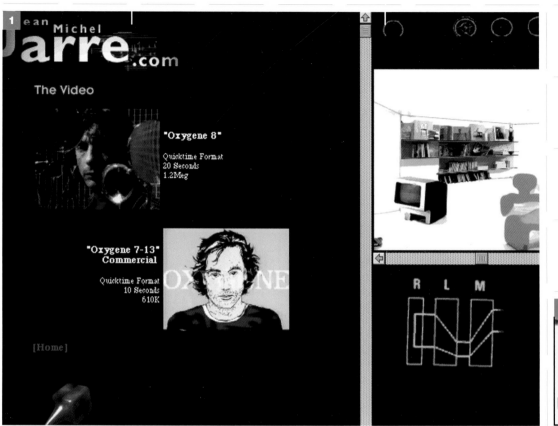

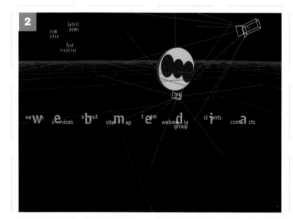

1 JEAN-MICHEL JARRE WEB SITE FOR
SONY MUSIC EUROPE

2 WEBMEDIA'S OWN WEB SITE

3 READER'S DIGEST WEB SITE

4 TIME OUT WORLD CITIES WEB SITE